In Bed With Cows

Andy Frazier

In Bed With Cows - © Copyright 2012 by Andy Frazier
Published by Chauffour Books
eBook edition 1.00 – August 2012
www.chauffourbooks.co.uk

Author's note

For 3 years now, I have earned my meagre living as a writer – lovingly supported by my wonderful better half, Wendy, and during that time no less that 20 books have passed through my rapidly typing fingers.

For most of that period, I had never really had a plot or even known what was going to happen to my characters until the words came out in front of me. I became a child again, passionately writing vibrant stories for children – as well as grown up children – every one of which I enjoyed, probably far more than my readers ever did.

During that time and all those words, I had one policy only.

Never, ever, write when I had a drink.

It stood me in good stead, having seen some of the doggerel that I had written under the influence - and that of others in similar states.

But I always knew, somewhere deep inside, that there were stories in me – true stories – that involved a little alcohol. Stories that are funny. Stories that maybe it takes a little alcohol to recall, and a little more to hear.

So, against my better judgement, I have rescinded the pledge – remind me to tell that story later, about Charlie looking for the pledge, it's hilarious – and taken just three weeks out to tell as many tales as I can, accompanied by a glass – or two - of red, as I sit in comfortable French sunshine and laugh.

Please excuse me if I ramble a bit, but hopefully you will feel and – if you close your eyes – **see**, my smiles.

My stories are about being in bed with cows.

I hope it works

Andy Frazier

I would like to dedicate this book to the legendary Captain Ben Coutts, for his encouragement to start writing.

I am indeed, a lucky laddie…

Andy Frazier

Prologue

Greetings!

There may be a few reasons why you picked up this title.

Perhaps its catchy name caught your eye, or you noticed it was about cows and you quite like cows – I can empathise with that.

Maybe it just aroused your suspicions?

Either way - you took a chance.

I am only too aware that a strange author with an intriguing new subject can often become irritating within a few pages, but please stay with me as long as you can.

Not that I am all that strange….

But, seriously, I thank you and will try and remember that you are with us on this journey back into the murky depths of my past. I sincerely hope you enjoy the bumpy ride.

However if, as I suspect, you have heard of or met me or, more likely, have a vested interest in cattle and the antics that accompany them on journeys to exhibitions where their handlers often get up to foolish shenanigans, then you may want to skip some of the more basic explanations of what happens - technically - to whom - with what.

Hello. Again!

Just for you, I will format the odd *technical* paragraph in *italic* text, so you can smugly skirt over these bits – with as much arrogance as you feel necessary – and just pick out the juicy bits.

Maybe you'll even get a mention. Who knows?

I can't guarantee that you will, though, but then again, I am not wholly sure who you are, am I? Unless you are that bloke I once shared a room with in the Rank Village in 1984?

Would it help if I added the odd mark in the margin where *sex* comes into the story? Like an asterix or something?

After all, you are probably reading this on Kindle, right? So no one will know what you're reading. And even if they did, it's a fairly bland title – a book about cows in bed? Not suspicious, surely?

Real cows and real people – and possibly drink.

It's not like it's porn or anything? Please don't be alarmed – the sex won't be with animals – well not the 4 legged ones anyway – and to be honest there won't be a great deal of it, sadly.

OK. Before we start, let's check if you *are* that bloke with whom I shared a room in 1984 at the Royal Show. Because, if you are, it is just possible that you know who I am – or was.

All I know of you is that you smelled of cows.

Stank, in fact.

And that you went to bed quite early and got up for work shortly after I staggered in drunk, in the small hours.

I really must apologise for what happened on the third afternoon of our co-habitation. When you popped back in to the room, possibly to collect your milking gown, and I was stark-bollock naked, face downwards on some bird I had met in the bar after judging. I guess you may remember what my arse looks like, probably better than my face, hmm?

And, for the record, it wasn't me giggling, it was her - whatever her name was.

Felicity, I think. She had sheep.

You really didn't need to pack-up your things and move out that evening. I am sure we could have worked it out – made friends, even? All stockmen together, and all that, eh? You could have extolled to me why dairy cows are all so thin, and in exchange I could have explained the basics of personal hygiene.

Still, thanks for the extra space. It gave me somewhere to lay out my ropes and leather.

And chains.

Chapter 1 – Stafford, England - November 1976

I mention England, because there is bound to be a Stafford in USA, somewhere. Possibly more than one?

Can't really blame them for taking our town names with them when they settled there, I suppose. Although, I fail to see why anyone would want to take Stafford with them? It's not very nice.

If I had upped sticks and left Stafford for the shores of the promised land, I'm damn sure I wouldn't have wanted to be reminded of it. Perhaps I would have named my new town, Newtown.

Or Shitehole…

Anything but Stafford.

Anyway, it was Stafford – the New Bingley Hall – and it was snowing like Christmas in a Hollywood movie, building up on the cars and lorries outside until they glistened like fairy cakes.

Anyone old enough to remember '76 will recall the long and much talked-about drought that lasted half that summer, throwing farming and crops into turmoil. I guess the snow was just a counter to that. Nature having a laugh.

Not that the long summer had bothered me too much. For the early part of it, I was still at boarding school, doing a few exams and then lounging about getting a tan at my father's expense. I certainly wasn't thinking about cows.

If I recall, all I was thinking about was Fiona Bufton.

Everybody was - because she had great tits.

In fact, she had the only tits.

Andy Frazier

We only had three girls at our school, with the grand total of two developed tits between them. Not a good average, really, when you think about it. Certainly not enough to go round. 150 horny boys and one pair of tits was a scandalously low percentage. Only 0.75% of Fiona's breast with our morning porridge!

Each.

Pitiful.

I am sure this single statistic provoked the biggest case of mass-masturbation since Lady Godiva had posed through Coventry without so much as a hair-net.

I was fifteen. In 1976, I mean – not when Lady Godiva was doing her equine-streak, that was a bit earlier.

The **New** Bingley Hall is so named because the old one burned down in 1974.

It was a quaint old Victorian purpose-built exhibition hall in the heart of lively Birmingham. New Bingley Hall was – and still is – a whacking great shed on the outskirts of Stafford, 30 miles from civilisation.

I'm sure they had their reasons. After all, this *was* the 70s.

Anyway, on this occasion, New Bingley Hall was toasty warm inside, despite the weather, as it was full of sweaty cattle and sheep all competing at the Birmingham (now in Stafford) Fatstock Show, and the reason I was there was that we had taken Freddy along.

Freddy was a Friesian. That much I knew.

And he was fat.

Boy, was he ever!

Stodgy globules of fat protruded out from him like

mole-hills, in places where they shouldn't, and his belly ballooned around him like a Zepplin, intimating that he had possibly eaten all his siblings.

Freddy was also as bald as my grandfather – all over.

Well except for his underbelly and the strange tufts sticking up in surprised fashion on his forelock that did little to disguise his horns – which were at least a foot long!

It has to be said that Freddy was quite a laughable spectacle, especially when it came down to competing amongst professionals.

Blame for the embarrassing physique of this creature could be purely laid at my father's door and could even have completely passed me by without ridicule, were it not that I was - somewhat unexpectedly - left to take charge of fat Freddy whilst the others all went back home to their comfy beds and left me sitting on a lonely straw bale.

Feeding animals was my father's forte. If an animal would eat it, he would keep on delivering. No wonder animals like him. Pigs, sheep, cattle, cats even, all ate far better than we did – possibly because they didn't have to endure my mother's cooking – and regularly took the accolade as the best beasts in our weekly livestock market at Kidderminster – with the exception of the cats who sat around by the back door waiting for more.

Have I gone far enough into the story now to bore you with some background detail?

No?

You're probably right. I'll save that for chapter 2, or maybe - if you're lucky - leave it out altogether and just stick with the fun stuff.

Right! Back to me and Fat Freddy in the middle of nowhere on a winters night - in a shed big enough to store a dozen jumbo jets.

Well, firstly, it was a surprise. My old man had phoned the school *head*-man and suggested that I have a couple of days off, to go to a *cattle show* which might broaden my education. Dubious that I was capable of learning anything more than how to peek through the stretching blouse-fabric of Fiona Bufton's cleavage during tea without her noticing, Reverent Vivian reluctantly agreed and afforded me Monday and Tuesday out of school on the understanding that I would write an essay about my exploits on my school return.

Sorry it was late, Sir - about 35 years late to be precise. But here it is.

Cattle shows are just an excuse for an annual piss-up.

There you go, head-master!

And to you, seasoned cattle show exhibitors, I said I would warn you when I was writing technical information for the uninitiated. Need I explain more?

Yes? Really?

Oh. OK, then.

Cattle shows, especially winter ones, are when grown men with little or no other sporting interests, select their best animal – a steer or heifer, or lamb, or porker, let's not get too bogged down with the terminology – give it a wash and some extra feed rations, groom it like a film star and then drag it unwillingly along to a place where lots of other people are doing the same.

Which, in this instance, is a massive steel shed in middle England.

They then tie it to a rail and sit about drinking alcohol for a few days. Somewhere in the middle of all that, someone wins a few prizes and everyone claps, and then celebrates - with more drink.

To those not in the know, this may come as something as a surprise.

I wasn't in the know at that point.

But it didn't take me long.

I'm not sure if it was the endless pints of Brew XI, or my first real taste of whisky, but something on that very first night in Bingley Hall changed my life.

For the next 4 score years, or how ever many that life was going to furnish me with, I was set rolling on a mission. From then on, Fiona's ever increasing bosom paled into insignificance compared to the wanton, the drive, the desperation, infatuation, obsession and desire that arrived within me on that night…

For during that 12 hours of darkness I was to enrol on a career - I never chose it, I swear it chose me – that was not listed in the flimsy sales banter of the school careers office. Fireman, Soldier, Dustman, Politician or, if all else fails, Farmer.

No, to me, my destiny was a life of vice in the wonderful world of cattle showing.

On only my second night into this new-found career, as it happens, ***vice*** turned up in the shape of two strippers.

Hello – I hear you say – I thought this was a ***cattle*** show?

Well, yes it was, but in those days, showing cattle was a man's world, and men occasionally needed to enjoy a little of the high life when they were away from home.

Two slightly wrinkled ladies, one white, one black - not dissimilar to the testicles of poor Freddy down there in the cattle lines - hoved into view on a makeshift scaffolding stage in the Prestwood Suite function-room to rapturous and lurid applause. The fact that these two were probably moonlighting from their night-shift security job in a Stafford warehouse did nothing to quell the enthusiasm of a couple of hundred baying cattle warders – complete with a virgin one, goggle-eyed in the front row – as they waggled and waved progressively more of themselves until little was left to the imagination. Fortunately, as is oft the case at events such as this, a small hairy stockman arrived with a gallon of slick-oil intended for his prize-winning pigs, which the two ladies put to a use that would only nowadays be reserved for late-night viewing on pay-per-sniff TV!

Never, in the history of mankind, has a fifteen year old boy been thrown into such a deep-end from which he has irreconcilably emerged as a man – albeit one splattered with pig-oil on his best school uniform.

Needless to say, Freddy won no prize that year and I almost shed a tear as he was heartlessly carted off by a stout butcher wearing a brown smock and a demonic grin.

After leaving school the following summer, having never quite been fortunate enough to compare Fiona's fairly average frontage in close-up with the monumental dark-skinned boobies that had been briefly wrapped around my cold ears the previous winter, I was to return to Stafford in November with Freddy II, a slimmed down, dehorned and reasonably behaved version who took home a third prize ticket.

Sadly, that year the evening entertainment at the stockman's dinner, under request from the club chairman's wife, had now been reduced to a singing duo so moustachioed and bland that a large majority of the audience had retired back to the stock lines for a game of cards before the end of their first tune.

Chapter 2 – Shrewsbury, ENGLAND, May 1978

Yes, we're still in England, and will be for some time yet.

Thanks for staying with me. I hope the horrors of a seventies permissive society didn't influence you to judge me too much. Those sorts of things happened way back then. Thank God we had Mary Whitehouse to clean it up…and Abba.

Shrewsbury: a rural city steeped in history, squatting with a leg either side of the river Severn, fiercely protecting it before it ventures into Wales. Or is it leaving Wales? I forget. No one could blame it for the latter.

The Shropshire and West Midland show was, and possibly still is, the first event on the County Show calendar when it usually rained – except when it snowed – in mid May.

Buoyed with the dizzy success of winning a yellow third prize rosette from a *fatstock* show, in I swanked to Shrewsbury with this year's new bovine contender ready to kick ass.

Little was I to know that my eyes were about to be opened wider than a shithouse rat…when one of the first things I met was Tattenhall Hublot.

To describe Hublot with any compendium of day-to-day comparisons would be quite impossible ….he was just the biggest, shiniest, fuck-off creature I had ever seen outside of Wildlife on One! I loved him. Next to him stood his son, the magnificently named Impeccable, who was no more than just another young Charolais bull, lining up in a stall next to mine.

Now to cattlemen the world over, this is like saying, I once teed off with Gary Player or traded ideas about domestic computing…with a nineteen year old Bill Gates.

Little did I know that this Impeccable living legend was going to be….a *legend* …for a very, very long time.

Furthermore, the stockman in charge of Hublot took heart with my cattle-showing enthusiasm and asked me if I, yes me, would like to accompany the great beast into the Grand parade. As it happened, we became friends and, later that year, I once again walked behind that same mammoth of a bull when it won the Burke Trophy at the Royal Show, for the second year in succession, only one of 2 animals ever to do so.

But anyway, I digress.

Or maybe I need to add some *italic* facts in here?

Yes?

OK, then. But not much, or my terminal shit-kicking readers will dose off and start slavering.

Charolais cattle come from somewhere in France, over towards the skiing end. They are pure white, freaking huge, and were– in 1979 - quite new to British shores. Since then, some say, they have cemented themselves as one of the world's most dominant breeds of cattle and **Tattenhall Impeccable** *has been a household word in the pedigree cattle register for over 30 years.*

It may also be noted that, at that time, the animal that I was exhibiting was a mere crossbred steer – that is to say it had no balls, and parents of mixed origins.

Stop it.

Even the most un-pc of you shouldn't be drawing any analogies to world leaders!

Actually that weekend in Shropshire introduced me to a few things, another of them being Bedell Maurice, an imported bull from the Limousin region of France, who went on to form the backbone of another breed that was to rival the Charolais from then until now – whenever now is.

A historical event, really.

Hublot beat Maurice in the play-off, as it happens, in case you're interested.

Anyway, this story.

After a few shandies in the stockman's bar, I settled into my sleeping bag amongst a couple of bales of straw and two or three of the most influential animals that the world cattle industry was to see for many a year. Quite cosy we were. I would like to announce a revelation that Impeccable snored like a wounded bison, but he didn't; not to my recall anyway.

What I was awoken by was something nearly as big. It wore a flat cap, boots big enough to surf on and swore like the profanasorous.

"Get up, you lazy c*nt…" were the first words Fred Harrington ever said to me. I quietly told him of this at his funeral some 20 years later.

Quite used to being awakened by aggressive drunken men in the middle of the night – it's surprising what you become accustomed to at boarding school – I obeyed and clambered to attention.

"…this f'ing thing yours?"

Almost honoured that *anyone*, let alone a staggering drunkard, might think this scrawny spotted teenager foetaled up in a sleeping bag may be the owner of such a magnificent creature, I chipped in that they were *all* mine, the whole damn lot of them, and would he, perchance, like to buy them?

In hindsight, it probably wasn't the best response I

could have proffered.

"F'ing foreigners should never be allowed in this country!"

It crossed my mind that maybe this was Enoch Powel's brother.

"Should all be f'ing shot, f'ing French bastards..." All his life, Fred was never a man to pull his punches. "Look at this high tailed c*nt?"

In my mild confusion I was none too sure what a high-tailed-c*nt was but assumed he was referring to one of the animals rather than me.

"Must 'ave eaten a whole f'ing store of cake this year..."

Unsure whether to call the police, Bayston-Hill hospital for the mentally unhinged or just anyone bigger that five foot seven, I cowered somewhat in my straw bed. But then foolishly I couldn't prevent my mind from imagining this herd of huge white animals in a cake-store and struggled to withhold a giggle.

"Grass!" The big man coughed for a while, leaning on a wooden roof-supporting post so that the shed coughed with him. "F'ing grass! Proper cattle should eat f'ing grass."

He did have a point.

This still being the seventies, my recent boarding school upbringing suggested that some grass may do this big man some good as well, perhaps calm him down a bit, but thankfully I kept this opinion to myself.

"Now Fred..." Out of the darkness loomed a man of equal size to big Fred, making me feel even smaller than my gangly stick-like frame.

It's funny how people say – NOW. Maybe it's a local thing, somewhere?

"Now – Fred!" I was hopeful it wasn't an instruction for Fred to do something. Like kill me, for instance.

"Prowler – you c*nt!" It wasn't too long before I found out that, to Fred, everyone was a c*nt.

"Thought we'd lost you."

"Cattle s'no fing good unless they 'ave a white head. More fing 'erefords in the world than all the other cunts put together."

"Bye Fred," I muttered as Prowler led Fred away, declining to remind him that Charolais did in fact have a white head, technically.

"C*nt," he replied, as if reading my thoughts.

I suppose if this is just a story about a young me, sleeping with cows, and then a mad old man stumbling along and swearing a bit, it might be mildly amusing to some? Maybe not?

You see Fred was entirely within his belligerent rights to be unwilling to accept this influx of competition to his cattle-breeding livelihood with the importation of these huge greedy beasts. What was wrong with what we had? The passion that big Fred emanated that night was something that many folks can relate to, that of change and the uncertainty it brings. And jeez, that change was happening so fast, it tripped up a lot of very clever people who dug in their heels.

Later that year, I was to join the Hereford cattle stockman's club – a group of men who worked with the great Hereford cattle race – men so proud of their breed and its origins they would unite together – usually for a few pints and a steak'n'kidney dinner – in the name of tradition.

Sadly the continental cattle did hail forth in multiples soon after that event and traditional breeds such as the Hereford declined almost to extinction. It makes me feel old to admit that I was there when it all started. It's almost like knowing someone who fought in WWII.

Fortunately, things have gone full circle and the 'old' breeds are back in demand once more. Strange really. It's like bringing back ration books and Vera Lynne, only with a plastic cover in digital format.

Chapter none - No more chapters

This book was never meant to be a diary or autobiography. I hate those – and I read plenty of them.

Either they're written by someone who is now famous and you want to skip through the part when they weren't.

Or it's someone unfamous, like me, categorising everything into years, decades, ions, to stop the reader getting confused. Start at the beginning. Finish at the end.

Maybe everyone dies?

Well, this isn't that type of book and if it was, perhaps our **clean** reader - yes that's you without the shit on your wellies - maybe he – or she – would skip to the end, just to see if I did get the girl, or win the prize, or even live the whole book out without it being finished off by a ghost writer – no pun intended!

I don't like that format so I am going to create a format of my own. I can do that.

Now.

Statistically, if you have reached chapter 2, you will make it to the end of the book, or at least past the middle. Thanks for staying this far.

I could bore you now, with things about my childhood, and my family and places I have been… even my pets. And you wouldn't leave. Not yet…

But I won't.

And now I no longer have any chapters, you won't know when I am suddenly going to add that in, will you?

It's just a game really.

I promise I won't cheat though

I don't like cheats. They never prosper.

I caught a man cheating, once. When I say I caught him… I exposed him, but in the end I backed down and let him have his victory. We both knew it was hollow, after that. Once you step over that boundary to reach your dream, the dream fades. I'm convinced he found that out.

Have I mentioned Smithfield yet?

No?

It's probably time I did.

If Bingley Hall was the place that set me rolling on a career in cattle showing, then Smithfield is the place where I had the most fun doing it.

I'll mention it soon. All in good time. You'll be fed up with reading the word Smithfield by the time you finish this book. If you finish it….

Anyway. This man. The one who cheated. It was with sheep, and he's dead now.

So let's move on.

No. Let's move back. To Bingley Hall again. Because there are almost enough stories emanating from that one building to fill a chapter with giggles to keep us through till tea-break.

One year I had a friend helping me out who, it has to be said, was – and is – as memorable to anyone who meets him as, say, 20th July 69 or – for your younger readers – 911. As this chap is now an upstanding member of the community I will spare his hide and just mask him name – as Rhino. The reason for this will soon become evident.

On our evening's retirement to the ever-comfortable straw-bale bedroom in the back of Bernie Birch's cattle lorry, Rhino announced he was hungry. Him being a portly chap, this happened quite frequently and usually required fulfilment within minutes.

Unfortunately, at this small hour, no fodder could be found to remedy his rumblings, despite our frantic searches.

That is until, like a manna from heaven, he spotted a sign.

Saying **ROBIRCH**.

Now bearing in mind this was a meat exhibition, it didn't take Rhino's seven inebriated brain cells long to decipher that behind said sign were possibly a drunken-farmer's Holy Grail.

Before I could utter the words – 'I'm not sure that's a good idea…' – Rhino had started to charge.

Did I mention he was a rugby player? A prop forward to be precise…ex-army at that.

By the time he hit the door, head down, this 19 stone lump had reached warp factor 10 – or possibly the sound barrier – only slightly off course. Missing the lock and the hinge for which the idiot had been aiming, the poorly constructed plywood panelled door never stood a chance as Rhino entered Pork Pie heaven – head first.

Now anyone who has ever read any Winnie-the-Pooh books will already have this mental picture cued up of what happened next. Unable to free himself from the yoke of splinters that now held his head fast, the slavering beast was now faced with a room stacked full of enough sausage rolls and pork pies to feed an entire regiment on one side of the door, and his arms on the other. Behind his arms, his arse stuck out in a highly kickable position, and behind that stood myself, guffawing with laughter so much that I was rendered completely incapable, despite Rhino's roaring.

Eventually, I managed to compose myself enough to boot him up the backside so hard that he finished the demolition job and left a Rhino-shaped hole in the woodwork. As we scampered off carrying enough sustenance to see him through the night, leaving a telltale trail of blood and pastry crumbs, we could hear the heavy boots of security guards clattering in from the other direction, who then stood gaping at the hole and scratching their heads.

The following day, an 'incident' was reported where possibly one of the cows had got loose during the night and taken a wrong turn! To this day, I believe that will still be on record somewhere.

Have you ever heard of chair-racing?

No?

It was quite a popular nocturnal sport – for a few years in Staffordshire in mid-late 80s. I am not sure who invented it. Me – possibly? Or maybe Piccolo Pete.

You know, to this day, I never got around to asking Pete why he was called Piccolo Pete. There is probably a logical explanation, although I doubt it.

After the stockman's dinner had finished, on one of the years where we didn't have strip-tease to entertain us, we decided to have an additional party, invitation only, in the centre of the main cattle show-ring, sometime after midnight. I am not sure who WE was, but at least 20 of us pulled up the usual furniture required for such an impromptu event – a dozen bales of straw and a bucket of water. The water was for the whisky, for those wimps like me who didn't take theirs neat out of the bottle.

These were hardened men.

I kid you not - I have watched two grown men have a bet on who could down a bottle of Grouse exhaling the least bubbles. Try this with a bottle of water and you will see how hard it is, let alone 40 degree proof scotch. Kids don't try this at home.

Anyway, there we all are sitting ring-centre, chewing the fat. Normally it would evolve into singing - something which fortunately boarding school had left me reasonably accomplished at. Sometimes it was in Welsh – eugghh, phlegm everywhere. I am pretty sure it was Piccolo who set the first challenge: of which of us could sit backwards on a chair and - hanging on for grim death – bunny hop the thing up to the far end of the ring and back. What a hoot, especially after a few jars.

Well, stockmen – *all* men perhaps – are competitive creatures and before you could say 'this may be dangerous', further challenges had been laid down.

By the following evening, we were under starter's orders, a dozen or more of us, lining up – again after midnight - complete with chequered flag and a pile of chairs nicked from the Prestwood Suite, pawing at the ground until the flag went up.

Can you imagine the chaos?

Let alone - the noise?

These were grown men, for god's sake! Doing a full lap of the ring, like some kids-school sports-day sack race!

And I won – I won!

About the only bloody thing I ever did win at Bingley Hall to be fair, but victory, none-the-less.

Hell, were there some sore backsides and stiff thighs by the next day. And a few casualties - both human and wooden.

From then on, for a few years anyway, the midnight chair-race at Bingley Hall, late November, became as big an annual event as the coveted prize of the supreme championship itself. We even handed out rosettes!

I don't think I ever won again – Mervyn Bradwys had me well marked! That Jim Bloom, he was somewhere in the mix, too.

Going back to the earlier subject – see I told you I wouldn't conform to timelines – Rhino featured yet again. Thankfully, not as chair-racer – the Prestwood Suite chairs would never had seen him get more than two yards – but as a sleeping guest in that same lorry.

Memory escapes me of exactly how many pork-products we pilfered that night in the name of alcohol, but let's say it was more that a couple. Having satisfied his monumental appetite, said chap snored off to sleep, as did the rest of us.

Sometime before daylight, a few dozen pork-pies protested that it was getting a bit crowded within Rhino's stomach and called, loudly as I recall, for immediate release. Stumbling over us in just a pair of briefs, he headed down the lorry ramp and out into the bushes to obey the call of nature, if you get my drift. After some screaming and yelling, the same man arrived back 10 minutes later, wearing just the elastic of the above garment and an embarrassed grin.

When quizzed on the matter, it transpired that, after relieving a heavy load, Rhino realised that there was no toilet paper provided in these bushes but fortunately, on looking down, noticed some material right there on the ground by his ankles.

'How convenient?' thought our hero, as he reached down and grabbed the cloth, omitting to notice the word 'y-front' on it. It still tickles me to this day to imagine the vision of 19 stone drunk teenager ripping his own legs from under him and catapulting backwards into the bushes. Fortunately, he found a soft landing…!

Right! That's enough of that.

Are you still here? I am quite surprised after that sordid tale.

I will try and clean things up a bit. So did he, as matter of fact…but let's not go there!

Less than a week after Bingley Hall, came the main event. Smithfield.

I said I would mention it soon - start counting!

If Bingley Hall was a big shed, then Earls Court, London, was its sumo-daddy.

In a previous book, I have described the first time entering Earls Court in late November in intimate detail. The sounds and smells don't just hang within me, but within thousands and thousands of other men and women who entered that building, ever hopeful, ever sober, ever ready.

When I say ever sober – well. This book is starting to arouse the suspicions of not only the AA but medical science in general, were I to suggest that, even before many of them – us – arrived into the holy church of Earls Court at 6am, Friday, many of us already had the first party under our belt.

I can feel another chapter coming on. So go and boil the kettle – no better that that, grab a glass of something stronger – and let's start another verse.

What shall we call it?

Oh yes, I know. The greatest party on earth?

Andy Frazier

Chapter no number: Earls Court, London

Many of you, my friends, will have been to London. It's in England, not the one in America – I guess they have one tucked away, too. You may even enjoy the place. I don't. Not now, certainly. Too unfriendly, too fast, too everything if you ask me. But then, these days, I like to do things slower. Ask Wendy?

Shhh. That's a cheap gag.

Earls Court Exhibition Hall is vast. If you have been in it, please back me up to those who haven't. Nowadays, it is still home to the Boat Show, London Book Fair and a variety of other events. Sadly not for much longer though, as a little birdie tells me it is now owned by property developers, so the writing of its demise is fairly well scrawled on its grubby concrete walls.

In those days, though, for 10 days in late November, Earls Court housed its flagship exhibition, The Royal Smithfield Show. Anyone earning a living in that area, or the entire of west London for that matter, will advocate that during that week more money was taken in bars, restaurants, hotels and even the theatre, than any other week of the year. A few pubs, such as the Lily Langtree on Brompton Road, reckoned they actually took more money over the bar in that week than the rest of the whole year put together. That's a staggering thought – in more ways than one.

Because during Smithfield week, the farmers came to town.

If I may just turn back to you, the reader with the clean wellies, who probably lives in a small hamlet in rural England, for a second. Somewhere in the recesses of your mind, having watched countless episodes of Countryfile on

In Bed With Cows

BBC will be the old ditty, 'you never see a farmer on a bike'. I am not sure who started that rumour, but believe me, it's is an untruth.

I have seen plenty - in and around Soho in late November. But that's another story, which I may get to later, possibly with an astrix in the margin.

But to you, non-agricultural person, farmers are full of wealth and cash and assets. Driving fat cars and shiny tractors, they have to be surely? And they are mean – with their money that is, not mean as in Vinnie Jones or Pol Pot.

In some cases you are right, there are some very wealthy farmers, or there were back then, not so many nowadays. However, these top-of-the-range people are in a minority and many of them support an overdraft bigger than the national debt of many European countries.

No, your average farmer lives on what is statistically known as a family farm: never quite big enough to warrant a full-time labourer, never quite productive enough to maintain a black bank account, certainly never quite passive enough to take a holiday. Unless, of course, it could be put down to expenses.

Click - whirr. Now you're getting my drift. Yes, farmers took off for a couple of days, leaving their wife to milk the cows and their 6 year old son to check the sheep, while they went to town to do a little business. In their thousands.

And to the ones with a little bit more courage and/or imagination, if we're off to town, why not take a few cows with us. Just for company. In case we don't know anyone.

Much to the dismay of the locals, in late November, 700 cattle and 400 sheep rocked up in west London and the hullabaloo could be heard for miles.

Should I have put some of the above paragraphs in italics? So our seasoned stockman/woman could skirt over it, nodding in understanding? I have to say stockman/woman these days, because the number of females working within the world of livestock-showing nearly equals that of males, these days. And they are good at it, too. After all, they are the more creative sex.

Hello to you, madam. Please excuse the swearing.

But back in the eighties, most womenfolk – isn't that a lovely derogatory term? Womenfolk! No wonder Emily Pankhurst got a job in politics - Yes, back then, the ladies of agriculture stayed firmly at home holding the fort. Stoically the home-fires were maintained while their hubbies, and possibly the teenage sons, went off to do a bit of business.

Maam, may I just mention here that if you think you recognise any of the characters mentioned in this book as one of your kin, it isn't, OK? Before you go smacking him around his baldy head with your Kindle while he innocently lies snoring beside you, just consider that his days in London were a learning experience to make him a more rounder person. Mentally, I mean, not physically.

OK, I have bored you enough now with the old 'farmer comes to town' speech. Let's get me back to the late seventies. Sadly Freddy never got down to the old *smoke* to compete against other Friesians, although they did have classes for them, way back then. No, my new exhibit was called Alex, named, as it happens, after a seasoned rock-and-roller called Alex Harvey, who has long since died of drink and left a shining example to the world of how to party yourself into oblivion. Until now I never considered the irony of that.

Alex was a cross Charolais – no not cross like that! Might as well get that gag in early. A cross-breed. Charolais father, Hereford mother. In the fatstock world, the crossbreed is king. Or queen.

I'm not sure if it comes down to intelligence, probably

not, but one thing I have always been blessed with is the ability to learn, fast. By year 3 in my new found career I was already starting to compete with the bigger guns, especially those in Bingley Hall, England's premier fatstock show. Alex had won a prize in the crossbred class the week previous before he waddled in through those monumental sliding doors into Smithfield show, both he and I swirling our heads around in awe. I use the term waddled as, at this point, my father was still in charge of the feeding regime. We found our way to the stall with his name above it in bold letters and my heart skipped a couple of beats. Here we were, at the mecca of it all. The pinnacle of pinnacles. And we were ready, this beast and I.

This was Friday. Four days to sit and wait until judging commenced, on Monday. Hurriedly, I picked up a catalogue of exhibitors, eager to suss out the competition in Alex's class. As we had travelled down with the Hereford stockmen through the night, Big Fred included, we were one of the first to arrive in Earls Court, around breakfast time and the stalls around me were empty. To my horror there were 62 entries on our class. Sixty Two? That couldn't be right? And just about all of them belonged to Mac-somebody or other. Nearly all Charolais crossed Aberdeen Angus. I had seen a few Angus, they were no great shakes. The Hereford was better.

Have I mentioned hair yet? Apart from the aforementioned Freddy having very little of it? OK, cattleman, go to the bar and get the drinks in, while I explain to our uninitiated reader, he or she, the benefits – nee, the necessity – of hair. I'll put it in italics so you can ignore it when you get back. Mines a glass of sauvignon, by the way. Now. It wouldn't have been back then. Back then I wouldn't know a good red wine from a gallon of diesel. My how times change. Let's just say, I was a little naive in those days.

Statement: Hair is everything on a fatstock beast. Discuss.

Andy Frazier

Let's start with the basics. Fatstock animals – incidentally no longer termed as fatstock, possibly because it is considered politically incorrect to call someone fat or, more likely, fat is not a desirable product anymore. No more bread and dripping for us, in case we all have coronaries. Like Americans do. No, nowadays they are called Primestock. As in prime beef. You know, animals that we are going to eat very shortly. Basically, poor Alex was heading for a sharp hook directly after this event. I hope you're not a vegetarian? Furthermore, I hope after reading this book, you don't turn into one. I wouldn't want to be the cause of that. If you are, try and read on anyway, there won't be much blood. I don't want to lose you now.

I probably didn't explain that very well, did I? But I think you get my drift? These animals were all about meat. About being the right **shape**, *size, width to produce the best beef. Possibly, the finest beef in the world. Did you happen to notice the optimum word there? SHAPE.*

Imagine your next door neighbour's privet hedge. Every year – perhaps every week, if you have one of **those** *neighbours – he trims it into shape so that it looks square, and tidy. Box-like. He couldn't do that if it didn't have any leaves on, could he? It would just be bare twigs, all brown and see-through. Right, substitute leaves for hair. Now you're getting it. No real need to breed an animal the right shape, if you can do topiary. And that's what we did. The more hair, the better shape you could make. And when it comes to hair, fine silky smooth straight long hair, the Aberdeen Angus has the best there is. The Hereford, on the other hand, has curls.*

Oh, you're back soon. Not much of a queue, eh? Cheers.

I was just telling the other reader about how the Angus has the best hair. You'll agree, won't you? Unless you're English?

Even you, the unititiated reader… Wait a minute, can I give you a name? I have trouble spelling unititiated – see – and anyway I don't want to call you that anymore. It makes you sound stupid, and I'm sure you're not. And – and, here's the good bit – you're getting more initiated every minute.

Oh damn, now I need to think up a name for you. And that will probably offend you too. Let me see…. Charlie? That way you could be male or female? Or Alex? No, that would get confusing. How about Jacky? No, got a male/female spelling issue there.

 Like the French do.

I live in France, did I mention that? Everything here has to be male or female, even a cup and saucer. And the spellings are all different. Nightmare. No chance of sitting on the fence in French. I wonder about gays, though.

Anyway, I am rambling. So. Charlie, it is? That OK? Suburban enough for you? If you don't like it, just substitute your own name every time you see the word Charlie. Shame I couldn't sell personalised copies of this book, then I could just search and replace. You know, like <add-name-here>. But I can't.

Right, Charlie - I feel I am getting to know you better now - even you with little knowledge of the cattle world will know that Aberdeen is in Scotland. There is one in USA, it's huge, too – but we don't mean that one. So the Angus hails from north of the border. Scotland. Land of the thistle and Billy Connally - and men in skirts. Oops. Sorry, that just slipped out.

One by one, the Mac-somebodies arrived, dragging their weary beasts all the way from Scotland, each one wearing a hessian sack over its dishevelled messy hair. As they arrived, I ticked them off – no, I don't mean I gave them a bollocking, I – you know what I mean. They looked a mess. On having little else to do, Alex had already been groomed a hundred times by 11am. He looked the business. Mac-Dreary did not. This would be a breeze. I was already holding the silver cup in my hands, my mind doing victory laps around the stadium to rapturous applause.

Wrong!

I am not sure I have even been more wrong in my life. Apart from when I danced with a pretty girl called Isobel at a hunt-ball once, only to find out that she was in fact really called Brian and actually had a pair of hunt-balls of her/his own!

Duly the beasts were tied up and the stockmen headed for the Prince of Wales to refuel. And that pretty much took care of Friday. Obviously I went there too, and did my best to understand the language of the drunken Jock as they repeatedly took the piss out of me. No problem, thought I. Come Monday morning, your famous grouse won't be so famous then. Ha.

Then, Saturday arrived, all too soon. Cattleman/woman, you know only too well what happens on the last Saturday in November in Earls Court. Or did do.

Miracles. That's what.

Charlie, you think turning water into wine, walking on water, even England beating Germany at football rate right up there on the miracle scale? Not a chance. In the top 100, John Prescott living to the age of 65 might just squeeze in at number 99, with the other 98 places filled with magical animal transformations from the likes of Davy Smith, John Lascelles, Scott Watson, George Cormack and Ian Anderson, to name but a few.

My grandfather was a wily old bugger, and one of his favourite sayings was 'you can't make a silk purse out of a sow's ear'. On that day – I discovered that you can. And they did. By Sunday morning, there were more silk purses in Earls Court than in the Empress of China's handbag.

And by Monday, some of the silk had turned into satin, so gold threaded as if made by Louis Vuitton himself as a gift to the Queen.

In some respects, I consider myself lucky that I was usurped in such belligerent fashion by those highly skilled craftsmen at that event, and perhaps it has stood me in good stead. I realise now how naïve I was, and how much I had to learn. Had these men turned their hands to professional hairdressing of the human kind, Vidal Sassoon and his transgender buddies would have been out of business in no time. They were the first generation of highly skilled stockmen I had ever encountered. On that very Monday, Alex and I dismissed back to our stall with not so much as a second glance from the cattle judge in that holy ring of sand, I considered only one thing. If I was to compete at this level, I would have to up my game.

Thankfully, by the time the turn came for the next generation of skilled bovine hairdressers, I was amongst them.

Another Chapter – Earls Court, underground

Charlie, have you ever slept in dungeon? I have. For one week per year, for 15 years. Me and another few hundred like me.

Few people will know that in the bowels of Earls Court exhibition hall is a labyrinth of corridors and rooms, collectively known as the basement, albeit a bloody big one. To us, they were more affectionately termed as the dungeon: dormitory, restaurant, bar and home-from-home for the man – no women allowed – who took his cows on holiday to London.

We lived in 'A' block. It was grubby, plagued with rats and giant spiders, unbearably hot and stuffy; it smelled of mould and cowshit.

I have to say, hand on heart, it was the best and most pleasant place I have ever stayed in my life.

For 50 to 60 years, those dusty walls will have witnessed more japes and high jinxes than a wagon full of monkeys on acid. Characters, many of whom are sadly no longer with us, whose names read like a who's-who among the legends on the bovine epitaph. Many of whom should have been on the stage and even knighted – for their entertainment value.

Instant comedians – just add alcohol.

Whenever I even see the word Smithfield, my mind conjures up memories of the laughs we had in A block.

On the far wall, near the door were the Welshmen. Dai Bonks, Merv Bradwys, Winston Bowen and little Clive who was a bit hard of hearing. It was as though they had a rota as to who would be the brunt of the next crazed idea of how to

In Bed With Cows

wind each other up. I'm telling you, the Marx Brothers had nothing on these guys. Many a morning we would awake to find that Dai's bed was now raised up on top of a wooden crate, six feet off the ground, with him fast asleep in it. Or Merv's bed suspended from the heating pipes on the ceiling by 4 cattle halters. Each morning, the boys would regale tales of their visits 'up town' to a few pubs in and around Soho and the antics they would get up to with local working girls, all in the name of fun. Dai, a publican from mid Wales, was so good at communicating with people that within a couple of years, he had befriended the entire Earls court staff. They loved him. This came in exceeding handy as between them they regularly had deliveries of 'booty' from the bars and kitchens, accompanied by a note of thanks. Always on the look out for a deal, one year Dai brought an entire trailer load of Christmas trees with him, which I understand had been 'collected' from a Welsh hillside and, after decorating up the dungeon, the remainder ended up on a market on Petticoat Lane. This deal had been done via a few Earls Court security guards and a knowing wink. On another occasion, same said Dai managed to purchase a London taxi from someone's brother-in-law, which he drove back home to Wales and, much to his wife's surprise, rolled up in the yard and used it for a few years carting ewes and lambs from the lambing byre to the hill!

At the other end of our large dorm, was a kitchen and bathroom with at least 25 massive old china baths where, as we were 20 feet underground, the water pressure was so strong it could fill a bath to overflow with steaming hot water in under a minute and it was a regular occurrence to see witness scolding water flooding the entire room when the tap had been left on too long. When I say kitchen, this was just a wooden work surface with half a dozen gas rings, where many of us un-house-trained men would cook a lardy breakfast from the box full of supplies sent by worrying wives (or in my case, Mother) who were convinced their men would all starve once away from their care. Normally we would all pool our resourses and take it in turns to cook and/or wash up. There were however, as there always is, a few who never quite pulled their weight.

One time, my good pal Gary Owen from Abergele announced that he was suspicious that our supplies of bacon and eggs were disappearing from the cupboard at quite an alarming rate and possibly we had a thief in our midst. Ingeniously Gary purloined, possibly with the help of the ever-resourceful Dai Bonks, a mouse-trap and the – er - trap was sprung, so to speak.

I mentioned earlier that the Scots were – and still are – the ones to beat when it came to exhibiting and grooming animals of this nature. Back in Bingley Hall we had one exhibitor who was streets ahead of the rest of the English pack and who consequently dominated the show for most of the seventies, winning the supreme title 9 times I believe. His name was John Mansfield, who together with his vivacious daughter Jane, was one of the few who was capable enough to take on the Scots at Smithfield. But, John did have a secret weapon of his own; an auld Scotsman named Alan Cruikshank, one of the old breed who had been there and got the medals to prove it. Now, bearing in mind we are in the late seventies, all the topiary and hair-clipping was now done by electric clippers with a very steady hand. In years past, however, this was done with scissors, a long laborious job that took a cat's patience and years of practice. When it came to scissors, old Alan was **the** man. Eyes behind half-moon glasses, bent at the knees he would focus for hours trimming the tiniest of hairs until John's beasts would have a coat like velvet. God knows how he did this as, in the ten years I knew him, I don't think I ever saw him sober! No matter, he was a legend. That was until one morning he arrived to his duty with half a roll of elastoplast around his index finger, so wide that he would be unable to fit it through the scissors.

Gotcha!

I can't remember how John got on at the show that year, but I am quite sure his cattle weren't groomed as perfectly as usual.

At the far end of the dungeon, which housed possibly 40-50 army-type beds, were the boys from Sussex - Frank and his crew. These lads were rough, could out-swear all the rest of us put together and were usually the last ones in at night – if you can call 6am night. They were also very often the ones who broke the only rule that our dormitory was constrained with – by a big sign on the wall – NO WOMEN ALLOWED! Frank was not only a ladies-man but also never a man to let rules get in the way and anyway, it is possible he couldn't read. Frank, if you are reading this book, I didn't mean that. You obviously can!

Let's just say that giggling was often heard coming from the Sussex end. One year, I was awoken not just by the sound of female laughter, but also singing. Beautiful angelic harmonies hailing from the far end of the dorm. Had I died from alcohol poisoning and gone to heaven?

"When will I see you again…." they sang.

As my eyes focussed in the dim light – it was never dark in A-block – I made out not one but 3 burly black ladies sitting on Frank's bed giving verse. How he did it, I will never know, but that night Frank had manage to pull, and subsequently persuade to visit our dungeon, the entire trio of The Three Degrees! That is gospel truth. I believe Frank went on to marry one of them.

The bed that I chose for myself was always in the middle of the room between the talented cattlemen of Julian Hopwood and Phil Sellers, a name many people will recognise for his continued success with cattle to this day. Opposite us, slept Phil's Dad, the wily – and sometimes grumpy – old Sid. Having earned his living as a calf-dealer in

Derbyshire, Sid had more or less retired when I met him, but he was always a man quick with a tale.

In fact it was he who once told about a cattle judge who was so confused he: *"didn't know whether he wanted a shit nor a haircut!"*

I often use that line - I think it depicts absolute bewilderment, perfectly.

Then in his late 70s, Sid was also, partially deaf. Eh? Or at least he pretended to be.

I am not sure if you can remember, but back in the early eighties, when the Gas Board was sold off in one of Maggie Thatcher's madder moments of democracy, a national advertising campaign was run on TV and billboards everywhere. The strap-line was: *"Tell Sid!"*

We told him, alright. Poor old bugger. Just about everyone he met asked him the same question for an entire week. "Have they told you?"

"What? Eh?" He never did quite grasp the joke. Until we eventually managed to pilfer a huge poster saying TELL SID and hung it over his bed. As with all of us, he took it in good heart.

Sid always had his birthday during Smithfield week, and one year on his way down from the main hall above, my girlfriend and I decided to appropriate a nice pot-plant from one of the main stands and delivered it to Sid as a present. Chuffed to bits, he displayed it beside his bed with pride. But then, as the day wore on, some alcohol was consumed, as per. On hearing it was Sid's birthday, a few of the other's thought it was nice gesture to bring him a plant as well, despite him now being tucked up in bed at 9pm. One by one, they arrived, as the plants turned to shrubs and eventually to entire trees when just about everyone delivered Sid's presents, courtesy of the agricultural trade stands, until Sid's bed was no longer visible behind an entire forest which other beds had been moved to make way for.

When he woke in the middle of the night to go for a pee, poor old bugger thought he was in the botanical gardens! It was like watching David Bellamy fighting through the undergrowth in a Borneo rain forest. You had to be there.

Next morning, security was alarmed by reports of missing plants, and wind of Sid's underground nature reserve drifted towards their horizon. Fortunately, with enough smooth talking and a scoop of belligerence, Sid just about managed to keep himself out of jail and the plants were returned, unharmed.

There's an old saying that goes: 'what goes around, come's around…'

Not known to be the earliest riser in our dungeon, especially as the week wore on, I was awoken one morning, in only my second year at the show – 1979 – by a couple of wags telling me that my name was being called for over the tannoy system. Furthermore, that I had been summoned to room 202.

As my cattle buddies reading this will vouch for, room 202 was the serious end of the event. In my later years, I turned from poacher to gamekeeper, as I joined the Smithfield Council and toiled with the job of organising the event. Basically, room 202 was the organiser's office, run, in those days by the fearsome Wendy Taylor. Let's just say it was a place you didn't want to visit, if you could avoid it. A bit like Milton Keynes.

Bleary eyed, barely awake, I listened to Gary winding me up.

'Come Andy, you have to go there – right now!'

'Yeah, right, mate. Do I look one day old?' mumbled I, rolling over and going back to sleep. 'Couldn't you pull a better stunt than that?'

Then Julian arrived, who at this stage was already working as a cattle steward. He sounded more serious, so I believed him. Sort of.

Had they found a wart on my cattle? Was I caught on camera urinating in the cattle lines the night before? Maybe I had been reported for not feeding my beasts before 9am? It had to be something bad, I considered, as I stepped out of the lift on floor 2, quivering with fear.

"About time too," chastised her Ladyship. "You need to be in the main ring in 15 minutes for a presentation."

"A presentation?"

Were they going to dismiss me from the show in glorious ridicule in front of everybody? Hang me out to dry as a bad example to the others?

"Wear a white smock…and brush you hair…"

Back then, I had quite a lot of it. Well it was the 70s.

Intrigued and terrified, I made my way to the main ring, dry of mouth and stinking of last night's booze. As I arrived, so did a fanfare. But not for me.

All rise.. and welcome….to Prince and Princess Michael of Kent.

Royalty? For god's sake, someone find me a hair-brush.

And now, to announce the winner of the stockman's judging competition. In first place, Andrew James Frazier – aged 18.

WTF?

I had only entered for a laugh. A contest that we were all eligible to compete in, judging a team of cattle which were then sent for slaughter and their carcases judged by a veteran afterwards. It might sound barbaric. It probably was. But here was I, three years into my new found career, at numero uno; beating some of the most experienced stockmen in the land.

Though the haze of it all, I cannot remember what Prince Michael said to me that day, as he handed me a splendid shiny silver cup, but I do still have the picture, in black and white on my wall in the music room.

It hides a stain.

I never did brush my hair.

Chapter 5 – The Royals

Let's leave the dank atmosphere of London for a moment and travel around the UK a bit.

Otherwise it will all get a bit boring. Charlie is already starting to glaze over, aren't you? I can tell. It happens a lot.

At dinner parties, mainly.

A tell-tale sign when I am mid-flow with yet another anecdote about some drunken mischief somewhere or sharing a beer with someone famous, when guests start looking at their watches.

Yes, in my career – if you could call it that – I have met a few of the Royal family. It goes with the territory. Remind me to tell you about it, some time. The Queen Mum was my favourite – I loved her to bits.

But this chapter isn't about them. To us cattlemen, the Royals mean something totally different. To us, the Royal's are a threesome.

Will I get sent to the tower for using the word Royals and Threesome in one sentence? Possibly. Your Highness, if you are reading this, please forgive.

Hello. Maam.

To us chosen few, the Royals are – or were – events. Monumental events that we all looked forward to.

By the way, did you note that I had started numbering the chapters again? Clever that, eh? It will keep you on your toes. Because I might put them in the wrong order, just to check you are still awake. What a prankster I am? You have to excuse me amusing myself though. You see, I have heard all these stories before.

But some of them still make me laugh.

Except this one:

My first introduction to the Royal Show was after I left the family farm to join the Professionals. Somewhere in my obsessed brain I believed I was good enough at showing and grooming cattle that I could make a living out of *it* and nothing else. I would be both Bodie **and** Doyle. It was a big and probably foolish step, I would be the first to admit. Hindsight is a wonderful thing.

Around that time, a new breed was making ripples in the country, not just little ripples either, but big blue waves. Having exhibited the very first Belgian Blue animal to be born in Britain, the previous winter, I had picked up a few contacts in this up-and-coming breed through its chairman, creator and advocate, Tom Ashton.

What? You want me to elaborate on that? Don't believe me, Mr Cattleman/woman, that I showed the first Belgy? Well it's true. Said creature was a nine month old cross-bred calf called Blue-Peter - by the imported bull, Lulu. I took it to Smithfield where it was the youngest in the whole show, and won a second in the open continental class. Not a lot of people know that.

The main contact I hooked up with was affectionately known by his peers as Ron-the-Con. A very descriptive handle if ever there was one. Maybe I should have known better, but hey, I have already admitted my naivety. Ron was a likeable guy who lived on the Isle of Man as some sort of tax exile and seemed kosher enough to me. In order to keep his new breed of cattle in competition condition, he lairaged them with me for a couple of seasons, where I trained, fed and groomed them in preparation for a few of England's main shows.

The flagship of his small show-team was a wonderful cow called Fifi du St Fontaine. Well over a ton in weight, this big gentle beast was a class act and a born winner. Even in modern times, I think she would still have taken some stopping. However, she came with a sidekick - another cow, nearly as big but nowhere near as gentle. The rough with the smooth. The chalk to Fifi's cheese.

That would make a great book title, wouldn't it? The Chalk to Fifi's Cheese. Sounds like an instant classic doesn't it? I can see it on the shelf now, up there with Mills & Boon and Nostradamus Ate My Hamster.

Or perhaps on the shelf above, in the Erotica section. Except nobody buys paperbacks from the Erotica section in WH Smiths, do they? No, they all download it on kindle instead. It's true! Have you ever asked a woman if you could borrow her kindle and then watched her go all coy and conjure up a dozen excuses why not? It's because somewhere amongst her 200 books, there will be two or three porn ones. And I can guarantee it has a password to protect it. I'm telling you. Fact. And she doesn't want you to know her little secret. Anymore than she would admit to owning a vibrator which she bought at an Ann Summers party a few years back that gets through 2 sets of batteries per year.

Sorry, I digressed there. A little bit of procrastination, because I didn't want to hear what's coming next. This other creature, her name was Brisha and she was a fucking maniac. For 6 months I tried everything to calm her down - kindliness, starvation, total brutality, strangulation – nothing worked on the wild bitch.

Hmm, I just read that last sentence again - maybe I *should* write Erotica?! Note to self – next book to be called **50 *Shades of Blue-Grey***. A farming gag there – I won't explain it.

Despite my protests to Ronny that she was a liability, he insisted that we took her everywhere that Fifi went. Especially, to the Royal Show.

In Bed With Cows

Cattleman, you know what's coming, don't you? You're smiling already. Smirking even. Smugly glad it wasn't you.

Using every trick that I had leaned during my short career, somehow or other I managed to drag Brisha into the show ring without the aid of a Ford 7000, and keep her there long enough to receive a 3rd prize. I never said she wasn't a good beast – just nuts, that's all. In fact, I think she even beat Fifi on that occasion. But then came the Grand Parade…

Charlie, have you ever been grass skiing?

I wouldn't recommend it.

The grand parade is a necessity at any show. And it is just that. A grand parade of all the prizewinning cattle, led around in the most public place, the MAIN RING, so that the general public – that's you, Charlie – can cast their uninitiated eye over them, whilst encouraging their children to scream and wave flags/balloons/life-sized cut-outs of Wonder-woman etc.

At least, I think it was Wonder-woman, I didn't get chance to study it for long, as we passed it -   at approximately 200 miles an hour - like a world-champion water-skier.

Replace large powerful 500 horse-power boat with one ton of prime beef with the brain of a psychopathic axe murderer, and you might get an image – the same image I have had in my nightmares for the last 20 years – of the occasion. To be fair, I did hold on, white knuckling my way for nearly three quarters of the circumference of that vast ring of spectators. The grand parade is normally led by the supreme Champion of the whole show. We passed him in an overtaking manoeuvre that Jenson Button would have been proud of.

We might have even made a clear-round, were it not for the appearance of a giant TV screen in front of us on the

Andy Frazier

last corner. It wasn't the screen that was the problem though – it was what was on it. In 50 foot Technicolor.

Yes, you've guessed it.

Me! - just passing through the sound barrier behind cowhood's answer to Donald Campbell.

Just in case those people in Coventry couldn't see us first hand.

Bastards!

Why, oh why, did the camera need to single me out like that?

What happened next was pretty inevitable really. Seeing a 50 foot sized version of yourself travelling at warp-factor 10, does tend to cause a blip in your concentration.

Over I went, head-first.

To be fair to my younger self, and stockman everywhere, I did do the honourable thing. And hung on.

It wasn't wise, or clever.

Somewhere in my obsessed brain, I guess I must have felt that by hanging on, I could save face. You know - show that I was still in charge of this lunatic and protecting the public from her savagery - despite the fact that I am now being rapidly dragged along the ground on my belly like a Saddam Housain through the streets of Baghdad. Eventually, the grass turned to concrete, as the violent cretin managed to home in on the exit. Fair do's to her, she might have been madder than Charles Manson – or Marilyn Manson, for that matter – but she did have a reasonable sense of direction. Bouncing along on rough concrete on your head, as your arms are stretched out in front of you like a half-dead Superman isn't really something that anyone should endure for more than a few metres.

It was time to throw in the towel.

In Bed With Cows

And some bandages, a gallon of TCP, an industrial sized tube of germoline and enough elastoplast to rebuild humpty-dumpty.

I still bear some scars.

My only hope is that the archive TV footage doesn't turn up on YouTube one day.

Or worse still. On **Pets do the funniest things**!

Amongst our team of 6 Belgain Blue cattle was another animal with character, a young heifer who went by the name of Daisy-May. Unlike the psychotic Brisha, Daisy-May was not vicious, nor even wild. She was just a bit of a bully.

Whenever feeding time came around, she would barge the others out of the road with the strength and skills of a bulldozer. She could even manage to shift Fifi, who was near twice her size.

If we move West a little bit, one of the other main Royals was the national show of Wales, chronologically the last of the three. With its quaint setting amongst the rolling hills of Builth Wells, the Royal Welsh was – and is – a huge event on the social calendar for just about everybody in Wales.

I say was – and is – as there are only 2 main Royals left now, the Welsh and the Highland, as the Royal Show – England – failed to withstand the last recession, possibly due to negligent management, and no longer exists. In fact that is a lie too, as there is another main Royal Show, the Royal Ulster in Belfast, a unique event in itself that will get a mention later.

Anyway, millions of Welsh families would crawl out from the valleys and take their holiday at this great event. No Spanish seaside and buckets'n'spades for this nation, oh no. A week in a tent at an agricultural show was far more fun. What's more, the Welsh being welsh are extremely patriotic about their wonderful show – rightfully so – to the point where the whole thing is televised on national TV so that those unable to attend can get a look-see.

At the end of a scorching day, we are sitting in that little pub, just by the bridge; I can't remember its name but I think it has the letter L in it, a few dozen times. Earlier in the day we had been exhibiting our cattle and Daisy-May was beaten into second place by a heifer owned by Michelle Gardener and ably exhibited by my good pal, Pete Bodily. Accustomed to losing more than I won, I was reasonably gracious in defeat and shook Pete's hand after the rosettes had been administered. Daisy-May, on the other hand, took exception to not standing first in her class. Before I could say, 'watch her, Pete, she wants to be head-girl', D-M locked down into first gear and started to drive forward.

As many a science teacher will advise you, it is impossible defy the laws of physics.

11-stone-3 of me attempting to restrain 650 kilos of Belgian topside in with four-leg-drive engaged was never going to work-out. As Daisy put her foot on the gas-pedal, Pete's poor heifer moved sideways without so much as gaining a footing. Thankfully, there were some railings in the way or else she would have ended up in the River Wye.

So there we are, sitting in the LLLelLLwysslL pub with a pint of Brains that same evening, when the barman shushes us to silence, and turns up the TV. Today's coverage of the Royal Welsh Show is on.

Never have I witnessed a man spit out so much beer and then go three embarrassed shades of purple, as Pete did, when the opening footage of Wales' premier event showed one animal locked in dominating combat with another. In slow motion, the entire pub – no, the entire nation – saw Pete's heifer driven helplessly towards the railings, which toppled over like a line of dominoes as the poor creature fell upside down into a marquee full of flowers, with him still holding the reigns.

I have an idea, if you listen hard enough, you can hear the laughter emanating from that one shot still echoing around the valleys!

I don't see Pete too much these days, but I am pretty sure he has never forgiven me.

And I am damn sure Welsh TV will still have the footage of that one, unless he has broken in and wiped the tapes.

He did get his own back, many years later when he accompanied me on a trip to Canada, but that is still a few years in the future.

We never did take our team of blues to the other Royal, the one in Scotland and it was a year or two later when I turned up on that turf, this time with a pair of blondes.

Charlie – I may have painted the Belgian Blue in a slightly bad light over the last few pages, but to be truthful, on the whole they are the most docile breed I have ever worked with. And I have worked with plenty.

However, in my experience, and I can only speak as I find, the Blonde d'Aquitaine was right at the other end of that spectrum. I can honestly say, I have had more bruises from blondes that any other breed put together. But that's enough about my sex life. Ha! Cheap gag.

I know I will lose friends and receive so much hate email that the internet will come crashing down when I say this, but I am not a huge fan of that breed. The irony of this - and it is immense irony at that - is that I now live in Aquitaine, in France, surrounded by the horrid creatures.

Having made my mark amongst the Blues, the following year I was sought out by a man named Mark. He, in turn, worked for a man, whose name I won't relay, who had sold his farm to the Japanese who then built a well known car factory on it. Thus, this man, let's call him Woolly, was wallowing knee deep in cash.

Predominantly, Woolly was a sheep man. With the aid of the very able Mark Lewis, now one of my closest pals, he won every major championship in the land with his Charollais and Hampshire sheep, and his prowess at feeding show animals was legendary. He even eclipsed my own father at this, and the two of them met head to head many times in a number of sheep rings. But that's a story for another book.

Revitalised with an obscene injection of readies, Woolly decided he would like to branch out into cattle, and the Blonde was his chosen breed. If I was to be spiteful here, he was rumoured to be quite partial to a blonde or two of the human kind. A costly habit. But I won't.

At around the same time, an imported cow was doing the rounds and, having had three owners in 3 years, turned up for sale at an auction. If I just say that a more aptly named animal has never walked this planet or any other.

Her name was VOLCANO.

As in Mount Krakatoa.

As in Impending World Disaster.

Where as Brisha was undoubtedly a mindless maniac, Volcano was completely sane, in the same way that Stalin was, or Lex Luther. She just didn't like people - any people. To say she was dangerous was like suggesting that taking afternoon tea with Chemical Ali would an interesting gastronomic experience.

If she were human, she would have been locked away in Holloway prison – or preferably Alcatraz.

Are you getting the picture here?

Credit where credit's due, Mark did manage to contain the creature using some interesting techniques, the details of which I won't divulge. But still, to let this thing out into the public domain was a venture that even the mildest mannered Health and Safety officer, with a blatant disregard for the rulebook, would have surely prevented.

As it happened, her visit to and from the Highland Show passed without incident, apart from the odd beating-up of anyone who dared step within 3 feet of her stall. With the help of a little herbal medicine, she was exhibited in her class and received a prize for her efforts, albeit a bit bleary eyed at the time.

All in all, we had a good show with these two - the other Blonde being Loosebeare Connie, bred by that master-breeding family, the Quicks from South Devon who managed to win the junior class and go on to be reserve female champion.

Get to the point, Andy…

At around the time I went professional in the cattle game, another chap appeared on the scene, with a camera. Whereas my remit was to make animals look pretty enough to win the eyes and hearts of cattle judges, his was to preserve the moment on cellulite for eternity. His name was Peter. Still is actually.

After a long and tiring day of being groomed, polished and dragged around a show ring, many animals got kind of fed up with it and quite understandably wanted to return to their stall for a rest and a drink. The very same could be said about the stockmen.

So the appearance of Peter, just as you were leaving the ring to do just that, was enough to make any stockman/woman's heart sink. Don't get me wrong, Pete is a lovely chap…

I just noticed that it seems like all my friends were

called Pete. Charlie, you must be getting a bit confused by this? Yes, this is a different Peter to the other ones. Let's just call this Pete, Peter Picture.

Many people in life have a few self-confessed failings, none more than I. Indeed, were I were to list all mine in the appendix of this book, the print cost would go up by 20%. Pete, on the other hand had really only one. Well only one which I know of, he may have others in his cupboard.

And that was...that he was a perfectionist.

Good was never quite good enough. And as we know – well I don't, obviously – perfection takes time.

And patience.

Cattleman – maybe I should call you Pete as well, just to save confusion? No, only kidding. I already have a name for you, but I will keep it to myself if you don't mind. Anyway, you who has been there and done it - you can skip the next bit as I explain to Charlie about why and how we need pictures of cattle - to keep the industry going forward.

So it was that Connie departed the show-ring, complete with a handful of brightly coloured rosettes, only to be intercepted and requested to stand and have her photo taken.

She, quite justifiably it has to be admitted, didn't want to.

The art of photographing an animal at its best is not dissimilar to that of grooming and presenting it to a judge. It needs to stand with its feet in the right place, look in the right direction and look alert, because from that one picture, a lot of money will be made in the way of advertising the herd, marketing offspring and siblings, as well as selling semen.

Simple? Not!

Now, if it were human, the word SMILE would come into the

equation.

Or CHEESE.

But, unless you have been on some sort of hallucinogenic drug-trip, animals, in general, do not smile. Cannot.

So with cattle, the image required is that the animal focuses on something and springs her/his ears forward.

With Pete shouting out instructions, the weary stockman would spend ages persuading an animal to move her feet a fraction of an inch this way and that. For a calm and well behaved animal, this may take a few minutes. For a not so happy Blonde, fed-up after a couple of hours in a show-ring and a belligerently persistent perfectionist behind the lens, this may – and did – take considerably longer….like an hour.

'That's it…" he yelled, eventually, 'now get her ears forward..!'

The traditionally recognised method of getting an animal's attention is to call her making mooing sounds yourself. Yes, I know it sounds ridiculous, but it tends to work. One or two of us are fairly good at it. I suppose mimicking the creature you spend most of your waking and sleeping hours with does get easier with time. I could crack a gag here – but Wendy would slaughter me!

With Mark holding her firm, despite our fatigue, I stood in front of her, just out of shot.

'Meeeerrrrrrooooooooo….' called I.

Nothing happened.

In fact Connie's ears drooped lower than an 80 year old's joy-sausage before the invention of Viagra.

'Try a sheep?'

"Baaaaaaa…'

Still nothing.

'Rustle a paper bag, sing a song…anything!'

As all else failed, out of sheer desperation, I did something rather out of character. A deed that I had never previously done, nor will ever do again.

I performed a handstand. A quite credible one, to be fair.

It appears that Connie had never seen a grown man standing upside-down before and for that brief second it takes to press the shutter on a Nikon F1, up went the ears and the picture was taken. It's a good one too.

Unfortunately for me, so was another one taken, by my watching father. Not of me bang upside down, legs in the air with small change showering out of my pockets either - but of me crashing to the ground with my face in the dirt. Damn those instamatics.

As I let out a roar when my neck twisted sideways at an impossible angle, coupled with bays of laughter from a half-interested crowd, Connie took fright, dashed sideways and crashed through some railings sending them sprawling.

They say every picture tells a story, but the one Mark has on the wall in his lounge is now completed with this tale. The other one will remain in the vaults where it belongs.

OK, that's enough of the Royals for now. One story from each one.

No hang on, I did mention another Royal, the Royal Ulster. My Irish readers would never forgive me if I didn't add that one in. After all, it is one of the strongest shows of all, with Northern Ireland producing some of the finest quality livestock in UK.

It is also one the best parties I have ever attended. And

as, you are gathering, I have attended more that most.

So, as we skip over the water, let's get a feel for the Royal Ulster show. Well, one thing that sets it apart from the rest is that it is situated bang in the middle of the city. Yes, I know Smithfield is in the middle of London City, but this one is an outdoor event. Balmoral showground is a huge patch of land surrounded by urban dwellings. Sadly, not for much longer, as they have recently announced a move to a more rural location. I am guessing it is for financial reasons.

Anyway, likewise for financial reasons, I took a trip to Balmoral…

There is irony here, isn't there? Because we all know that Balmoral is also the name of the Queen's Scottish retreat. Charlie will be getting confused again if I didn't outline that fact. So let's establish, there are two Balmorals, a bit like there is more than one London and Aberdeen. So any references to Balmoral from now on are to the one in Belfast.

I have been to the other Balmoral though. Get around, don't I? Over the years I befriended a little old guy who was rarely sober, called Gordon. Gordon worked for the Queen on the Balmoral estate as a gardener. Being good with cattle, one of his perks was to accompany her Highland fold when it was exhibited at - guess where? Yes, you got it in one. Smithfield.

It's like a bad smell, isn't it? Smithfield. You can't shake it off.

Anyway, after using one of the Queen's heifers for a publicity photo, Gordon made a sweeping statement: 'If ever you're passing Balmoral, do drop in and hae a look at the coos.'

If ever you're passing Balmoral…? Who the hell passes Balmoral? It's in the back of beyond, tucked away in the middle of a forest at the foot of the Cairngorms.

Well, one day I was up that way. And I did.

Sorry – sorry – sorry. I digress. As usual.

And now we are all baffled to buggery.

Back in Belfast. Balmoral showground again. Got it? OK.

I was there to meet and set up a new venture in cattle grooming supplies for a man by the name of Bill Armstrong, a gentle giant of a chap that you wouldn't want to be on the wrong side of, and his lovely wife…Eileen.

Grooming supplies? I hear you say. I'll come on to that in a minute. Be patient.

While I was there I got chatting to a chap who was exhibiting a superb team of Angus cattle and ended up giving him a hand. His name was Bob Campbell - another of life's nice people. Having won a class with an outstanding heifer who was enormous for her age, I then, somewhat foolishly, agreed to get her photographed…..by Peter Picture.

See, it all ties in neater than matron's uniform, doesn't it?

Unaccustomed to the troubles that blighted Northern Ireland at around that time, as we were heading out from the cattle buildings I heard something rather alarming coming over the tannoy system. Something even scarier than being summoned to Room 202 in Earls Court.

It said, quite matter-of-factly, and I quote, word for word:

'Ladies and Gentlemen. A bomb has been reported on the showground in one of the waste paper bins. If you so wish, you may leave the showground by the nearest exit.'

Unquote.

A fucking BOMB!

Shit-the-bed!

And here I am standing holding a 6 foot heifer.

I can't leave the showground by the nearest exit, taking a big black cow with me, can I?

What to do? Should I tie her up somewhere and leg it. Leave her behind to get her extra-long legs blown off?

I know, why not tie her to this handy waste-bin….aarrggghhh… a sodding BIN! Right there!

Can you imagine the scene of blind panic?

Yes, you would expect so, wouldn't you? But this was a country and - more exactly - a city, that was used to bombs.

Now that sounds ridiculous, doesn't it? How can you get used to bombs?

But they were. Nobody even flinched.

'Calm down, boy,' soothed one passing stranger.

CALM DOWN! I swear that was what he said.

'It'll be a hoax. They always are..''

'How the bejeesus do you know it's a hoax. Any minute now I am going to be shredded into little red pieces, fluttering on the breeze of eternity - me and this cow here. And you just laugh it off?'

'Get on with ya. Sure, if it goes off in dat bin there, you'll not know a thing about it, anyways. So what's the point in panicking?'

'It's called self-preservation,' I reasoned with him, 'now, here, hold this rope will you, so I can leg-it faster than an Ethiopian chicken.'

'Quick…come with me,' echoed a familiar voice behind me.

It was Peter.

Sensible Peter.

Saviour Peter.

'The Main Ring. It's empty. So we can take a photo of the heifer, in there.'

'A photo?! Haven't you heard? Armageddon is about to kick off, and you still want to take a photo? Man, you really *are* dedicated.'

'No bins, Andy….in the main ring!'

I could have kissed him. What a genius.

We followed him at a canter, my leggy black friend and I.

Having already established dead-centre of that massive piece of grass, Pete calmed me down and we set about taking a photo of this big docile heifer, just the two of us, in a safe-haven three-hundred yards from the nearest bin.

How would we get her ears forward though?

Ah, yes - I know. An almighty explosion. That would do it.

A worthy and dramatic conclusion to this tale would be that the whole cattle-shed went up in a mushroom shaped cloud - but it didn't.

There were no more warnings. No All Clear either. The event just carried on as normal. Now that, my friend, is a conditioned nation - and probably the groundings for the peace process to-boot. If you can no longer scare the shit out of the general public by setting off bombs, then perhaps its time to give up.

Right let's move on before I start getting political.

Oh, wait a minute. There was one more Royal Show that I enjoyed. It was called the Royal Melbourne Show. In Australia.

Earlier in this piece I revealed my exploits with Belgian Blue cattle but I failed to add that Ron (the Con) had exported a few to Australia. Casually he mentioned this in passing – we were at Cheshire Show and had just won the supreme championship with Fifi, I remember it vividly – and suggested that he required a groomer to put them in their best clothes to exhibit at this event.

Me!

You could have knocked me down with a silk crochet hankie.

Excitedly, I phoned my wife, for we had married earlier that year, and told her the great news, that I was off on a jolly on the other side of the world and would she hold the fort while I was away. You can imagine how that went down?

However, I will recall some stories from my international trips later in this book under a heading called International Trips. No, don't flick through and find it already. Stick with me here for now.

No, not here. Let's do another chapter. Maybe tomorrow, after you have gotten some sleep.

Chapter 6 – Mr Groom

In order to fund my cattle-showing habit, I had set up a small business providing much needed products to the cattle industry.

Hair grooming products.

Charlie, this is going to sound bizarre and perverse in equal measures. I can see you now, flitting to the blurb on the back cover of this book, and reading the words TRUE STORIES and rolling your eyes.

Yes, it is true. All of it.

Cattle in the seventies and early eighties were groomed using ladies hair products, purchased in volume at extortionate prices from style-boutiques up and down the country – until I turned up.

To start with, it was just a minor operation, where I went to a couple of wholesalers and ordered a few things in bulk, at a discount, and then sold them on to a few of my mates.

On my original list, I had halters made for me by an old chap with nothing better to fill his time, which I sold for double their cost. Also I sourced the manufacturers of a couple of things, like combs, brushes and golf clubs and did likewise.

Did he just say golf clubs? Yes, golf clubs.

Charlie, if you have ever been to a cattle show, which I am guessing you probably have, you would have noticed that most handlers carry a long shiny stick with them which is used to tickle the animal under its tum to keep it occupied, as well as to move its feet, a-la the previous chapter. All it took was a finger-trip through Yellow Pages to buy a bunch of golf-club shafts and have a local welder fit a hook instead of a club-head on the end. They cost a few quid and sold for a tenner. Easy peasy

Every time I turned up at an event, it was a like a car-boot sale from the back of my van, as those who had lost, broken or left at home their vital tools of the trade would rock up and buy a few things, for cash.

However, it was the grooming polish that was a bit harder to source, not least because it was so damn expensive, even at large volumes. In the early days, a dog grooming product called Shaws Coat Dressing was mainly used – remember that stuff, cattleman? It had a most wonderful smell that got you high as a kite. Smithfield used to reek of it. In fact not long ago I came across a groomer still using it. He admitted it was nowhere near as effective as modern hair products but just loved the smell and, he said, it transported him back to those heady days in Earls Court.

See, I told you it wasn't just me that was obsessed with that place.

Boldly, I phoned up Shaws, negotiated a volume discount of 20% and flogged gallons of the stuff.

In the last chapter, I briefly mentioned my trip down-under. Well, while I was there I discovered that most of the grooming stuff those aussie guys used was imported from Canada, and I hastily scribbled down the names of a few on a the back of a fag packet.

Yes, Charlie, I did smoke in those days, like a damp-bonfire. I don't now though, so that's alright.

On my return I picked up the phone – no internet back then – and got sent a catalogue of stuff from Canada that was about to make my business a lot more serious – and profitable.

For one thing, the US dollar was two to the pound at

that time and, for another, here was a whole heap of stuff I never knew existed. After a few gabbled conversations, and with the aid of the Midland Bank, I put in an order for some products such as Mr Groom's Showshine, Doc Brannen's Black Magic and Sweet Georgia Brown. If nothing else, Americans are predictably creative when it comes to trade names.

These went down a storm with my rapidly-growing gathering of followers, as my list of specialist products grew weekly, as did turnover.

Next I purchased a second hand exhibition trailer, kitted it out with a set of old baskets to act as display holders, a few hand written posters and a roll of old carpet, and set course for the Royal Show, the following year. As I was unable to operate a trade stand *and* groom cattle at the same time, it was manned – well womanned, actually – by a daughter of a family friend, Emma Walker, and my wife's younger sister Katie.

Both in their teens, two prettier and more able girls it would be harder to imagine.

It proved to be an excellent move.

During the day, I would pop back the stand, to check if all was OK, only to find it surrounded by eager young stockmen drawn to these two like wasps to a picnic. During the evening, I was obliged to act as chaperone as the parties turned more raucous when fuelled with alcohol. A dirty job, but someone had to.

In fact, they didn't require much looking after at all, both more than able to beat off the advances of young suitors if they wanted to.

They revelled in it.

Business grew.

My next move was equally bold. I decided that in order

to track down more products at better prices, another trip overseas was required.

This time, to Canada.

Chapter 9 – A Wizard in Oz

I know, I said earlier I would call it International Trips, but that sounded a bit naff. Not only that, but if you did flick forward looking for that chapter, you wouldn't have found it. Ha.

I'm not really a wizard – it was just a pun.

And OK, I may have the wrong chapter number, but that was done to throw you too. And to amuse me, of course.

Charlie, have you ever sat on an aeroplane next to a horse?

I have.

When I look back, it was possibly one of the most bizarre moments of my life. There I was sitting at the back of a jumbo, flying from Sidney to Brisbane when I glanced over my shoulder to see a long face eyeballing me through a narrow door. After a double take, I glanced to the sinister looking man on my right, nudged him in the ribs and mentioned, like a bad ventriloquist:

'Don't look now, but there's a gig horse in the row gehind us..'

It was at that point, that I glanced down to his lap. Just momentarily. I am not in the habit of glancing at men's genitals, I will have you know, but this just happened. OK?

And there, in his lap, was a Smith & Weston Colt 45.

Unlike when faced with the prospect of a UXB in an open space, on a Boing 747 you can't really run very far. And anyway, at 33,000 feet, the doors were closed.

'G'day!' grinned my neighbour, holding out his hand.

'You wanna go and see Sox?'

Despite my mind whirring like a Caithness wind-turbine, I accepted his outstretched hand and shook it, with my mouth still hanging open. In case you're wondering, no, the gun was in his other hand, all black and shiny and killer-like. In fact, he didn't look unlike Clint Eastwood.

Had I inadvertently joined the set of Dirty Harry Down Under?

'In case he gets upset..' proffered Clint, by way of explanation.

In case HE gets upset. What about if I get upset? And start screaming!

'Come on, let's take a look at im…?' Clint undid his seatbelt and clambered through the small doorway at the back of the plane, with me following, still speechless.

There, in a large wooden crate stood one of the biggest shiniest horses I have ever seen.

'His real name's Sebastian's Diamond,' continued our film-star lookalike, 'but we call im Sox.' He nodded his eyes towards the horses two front feet, which had perfect white ankles – socks.

Sox neighed quietly and nuzzled against my cheek.

It transpired that Clint, whose real name was John Beddows, was a qualified vet who travelled with horses up and down the country like some sort of equine-minder. Sox wasn't too keen on riding in a lorry and today he was racing in Brisbane. As the lorry journey would have taken 12 hours, the trainer preferred to fly him there in just over one. Then he could rest and kick-ass on the track.

Blimey. What about the cost?

Pah. This is the horse world. It's like the boating world. If you can't afford to waste millions at it, then don't play the game.

Thankfully Sox didn't get upset, so relinquishing the need for John to pop a couple of silver bullets into him. This was indeed a godsend. What if he'd missed or, heaven forbid, the bullet had gone straight through and into the fuselage? Or the pilot?

Can you imagine the insurance premium? Must have been the size of a wealthy farmer's overdraft.

I never did find out if Sox won his race. I hope so.

Anyway, here we were, in the land of Oz.

Actually, the horse incident was near the end of the trip.

My first introduction to Australia was in Melbourne airport, sitting in my underpants.

Thank god I had put some clean ones on.

Continuously I have admitted my naivety throughout this book, and here is another example. On entry to Oz, you are required to fill in a form stating your purpose there. On that form it asks a few simple questions such as:

Have you been near any cattle lately? – Yes.

Have been on a farm lately? – Well, yes, that's where the cattle were.

Have you got any part of a cow with you? Like some hair or something?

A fool – oh what a fool.

'Would you step this way, sir?' were the very first words that a real native Australian ever said to me. '…and open your bag.'

'Aha. Can you explain this?'

'Yes, it's a comb, still with some hair on it from the last animal I groomed. And these are my clippers, and my work boots complete with cowshit on them, and….oh dear, I'm in trouble, aren't I?'

Two hours I sat in embarrassed silence in a windowless cubicle, as the entire contents of my hand luggage was fumigated, complete with my Levi's.

Here are three letters that will make a British farmers blood boil.

B. S. E.

Remember it?

Mad Cow Disease.

Mad people disease more like. Media hysteria, the likes of which we had never seen before. In 2 weeks it caused more damage to the British beef industry than rats and fleas did to 17th century London.

Unless, your name was Ron the Con.

Let me explain.

BSE was something that was known about in the British Agricultural corridors of power for a long time. The government knew about it too, of that there is now plenty of evidence. Medical science had raised alarms that in one-in-ten-million circumstances, there could be the tiniest possibility that it may affect humans.

But those long corridors have very thick carpets – under which to sweep such scandalous accusations.

The BSE crisis – for it was a crisis, albeit for the wrong reasons – hit UK's press in 1994.

I was in Australia – in 1989.

So were Ron's cattle.

Just 4 days after those cattle arrived, a government policy was drawn up, banning the importation of any live cattle into Australia from Great Britain.

Why?

Because, dear reader, of BSE.

You see, somehow, the Aussies had got wind of our underlying problem, 5 years before the UK press did.

Now that is some cover-up.

I agree, I wouldn't believe it myself, were I not there and witnessed the evidence.

So, our Ron hit not only the Jackpot, but the entire contents of the cash-tills in the casino.

Rumours floated around that t'was Ron himself who alerted the Aussies about UK's underlying BSE problems after his beasts were home and dry. On that, I could not comment.

No matter. Here were 5 pedigree animals from a brand-spanking new breed, that was taking the UK by storm. The only ones of their kind in the whole of Australia.

Cha-ching.

And do you know the sad thing about this?

They were bastards, each and every one of them.

When I first clapped eyes on them, in a rickety old shed on a cattle station beside the Victoria River, I could have cried.

This was the birth of a nation.

A new dawn.

Adam and Eve of the cattle world.

Where Eve was a dwarf with cross-eyes and Adam a cripple - with a stutter!

Furthermore, while I was drying my eyes, I glanced around to see fields upon fields of some of the best cattle I had ever clapped eyes on - each and every one of them with magnificent ruby-brown curls and a white head. This was a Hereford cattle stud, the likes of which I am proud to say I have walked on.

In the trees of this opulent outpost, kookaburras cackled as though laughing at me. In the sheds, behind a few gnarled wooden slats, worn smooth with centuries of competent breeding, cattlemen sniggered at me too. Real cattlemen.

In front of me, a stunted bull with one crooked back leg, amongst 4 narrow white heifers, blackened with dust, lice and despair, shamed my very soul.

Fortunately, a young jillaroo took a liking to my pommie accent and added a little cheer to my otherwise dull spirits on that first evening, as we sat and dined on prime beef – despondent about the job I had been brought here to undertake. I extolled to her my Grandfather's old adage about *making silk purses from sow's ears*, as she soothed my furrowed brow in a fit of giggles.

The next morning at day break, I took a trip with the local lads that I am also ashamed to admit to. We went on a Roo shoot. I am happy to say, I never fired a shot.

Oh dear. I got a bit down there, for a minute. Maybe I need a drink.

My round! A large whisky, I reckon, to warm those colder thoughts.

Right, where were we?

Ah yes. Magician – do thy best. What would Davy Smith do on a job like this? Turn tail for home, maybe? No, he would make the best of it. Do himself proud. Show these boys a trick or two.

And I did.

Three days it took me. Admittedly I did have one hiccup, where to treat the lice I used a pour-on medicine which then reacted with their thin white skin, causing it to blister in the sun. It was like Sharon on the beach in Torremelinos, all bright red stripes as I massaged aftersun into the poor heifers' backs. It wasn't their fault, poor cows.

By day 2, I had taken pity on these unlucky dishevelled creatures, as I rallied around to impress the natives. It did the trick with the Jillaroo, anyway.

Next, I shaved them bare. No more tufty dead hair that was never going to get clean, let's see what's under it. It was a brave move and sometimes fortune favours he who takes the initiative. This did raise an eyebrow with the hardened old cattlemen as wisps of white hair fluttered by them on the breeze.

'I thought you only did that to sheep,' one said, but I was beyond caring. Here was a brave new world, so let's rewrite the rulebook.

When the stock lorry arrived on Thursday morning to collect my entry for the Royal Melbourne Show, we were as ready as we were going to be. At least the cattle didn't have a hang-over from the night before. Unlike me who had gone with the lads for a farewell drink to the nearest bar, some 40 miles away, and got rather hammered.

By dusk, we were rolling through the streets of Australia's second city, marvelling at the sights and speed of it all. By 8pm, the cattle were tucked up in their stalls and I went in search…of a party.

On a brief stop in Hong Kong airport's duty-free shop, I had purchased a free ticket to just about any social gathering on earth - a 2 litre bottle of Gordon's gin.

For £2!

I can see it now, glass handle built into the bottle, as the farm-boys in town passed it round swigging it over their shoulder. 12,000 miles from home, I have never been made more welcome.

But.

They hadn't seen my cattle, yet.

On my way out from the party, a few sheets to the breeze, I literally bumped into a man that I recognised. I knew him because he was one of the stewards at Smithfield, a quite short smartly dressed man named Tom Brewis. Unfortunately he didn't recognise me, but then maybe that was a good thing as I was perhaps letting the British side down a touch, in my inebriated state. Maybe he did, but pretended not to. Whatever. We had a short conversation and I went on my merry way.

Earlier that evening, I had fallen in with a gang of Angus breeders and, as my own cattle were not due to be exhibited for a few days, they asked me if I could lend them a hand the next day.

Cattleman, can you see what's coming next? You know who Tom Brewis is, don't you?

Yes, as I was kitted out with the biggest cow I have ever seen, the penny dropped with me too.

Charlie, my apologies if I keep seeing the biggest cow ever, but it will stop here. Cows just do not get any bigger than this one. It was of Canadian origin and measured frame-score 10. To elaborate a bit further on this, frame-scores are a measurement of how tall an animal is. British cattle are not measured by height, we prefer to breed ours a little thicker. In Canada, however, it is all about size, size and more size. The taller the better. If they could breed one as high as the CN tower, they would.

Andy Frazier

Did you ever see a fat man, 7 feet tall? No? Quite. Basically, with animals, as with plants, buildings, even stick-insects, the taller you go, the narrower you become.

Uhum. Stick-insects? Yes, that about summed up this cow, actually.

She *was* 7 feet tall and towered above little me, who is only 5-9, in my socks. No, I wasn't just wearing socks, that was an analogy, but being quite small, I did make the cow look even bigger. That must have been why I was offered a chance to show her in the ring.

I *was* a bit taller than the judge, though, as to my horror, I saw him as we neared the ring. Yes, you got it in one. It was our Tom. Who had come all the way from the Borders of Scotland to judge the Aberdeen Angus classes. And here I was, stitched up like a smoked-herring - the only British person in the whole of South Australia and I am about to parade a giant beast for my fellow countryman to judge.

Talk about how to make friends and influence people! Seeing the tactic from an unscrupulous angle, the other exhibitors would have lined up to put the boot in – and who could blame them. I would never be able to set foot in Oz again. And I quite liked it there.

Fortunately, I persuaded the rest of the team that this really was a bad idea, and could prove extremely unhealthy for me. Thankfully, they saw sense, and the task was handed to a girl who was half my size.

Still wiping my brow from the nearest escape I have ever had from crucifixion, I witnessed the ridiculous spectacle of this midget exhibiting 15 square-metres of shiny blackness from the sidelines. Inevitably, the cow won her class. I had just declined the chance to show a winner at a Royal Show, not something I have done often - but it was definitely the right move.

In Bed With Cows

Meanwhile, back in the cattle-shed, blue and white was the talk-of-the-town. Ron had printed 5000 leaflets - which incidentally I had carried from UK as hand-luggage, only to have half of them confiscated at Heathrow because my bag weighed 180 kilos – waxing lyrical about this new breed.

'The MUSCLE of the FUTURE', said the strap-line.

In their stall, our five closely-cropped exhibits stood forlornly chewing their cud as I, Mr Salesman, proffered a leaflet to anyone who wandered by in an Akubra and Driazabone.

I had my patter ready.

Over the years, many times I have been told I am a good salesman. I suppose I had picked up a few tips, selling my grooming wares at shows, but I would hate to think that I came over as a salesman at all. Apparently, it's my enthusiasm for whatever I'm selling that wins through – so I'm told.

Well, imagine a salesman selling you double-glazing – that didn't work?

Would you buy it, Charlie? Or maybe you would see through his false smile and insincerity?

'G-day, what's this then?' would be the common response.

'Oh. Hello, this is the latest new breed that is about to sweep the world by storm.'

'A pom, eh?'

'Yes, I am from England.'

'Most poms are.' I laugh pathetically at his joke.

'So what's so good about this guy here?' Points to the bull. 'A bit bald, isn't he? Jeez, don't they grow hair in pomland?'

'He's all muscle. His offspring will weigh approximately 20% more as yearlings than your local Hereford breed, giving you extra profits of x-amount.'

'I see.' That got him. He's hooked, already, I can tell. 'Let's see him walk then…'

'Walk?'

'Sure, a bull's got to walk - to serve the cows. Where I come from, it could be 2 miles from one cow to the next and maybe ten to the nearest watering hole..'

'Errr. He's asleep just now. Maybe later…'

Repeats request agitatedly.

'Err, he really is a bit tired, actually.'

'Look, are you going to promote this breed – or what?'

Dejectedly, I untie his halter and out hobbles our bull, his hind-heel clicking like an empty revolver and his right front leg swinging in an arc so wide it takes out a row of by-standers as we pass. By the time we get 100 yards, he wants to lie down again.

'You gotta be kidding, right?' Laughs uncontrollably and then looks around. 'Am I on Candid Camera, somewhere?'

And so it went on, for 3 long days.

Never, in my career with cattle or any other, have I been so humiliated.

Ron did do well out of them, though. If you thought I had sales patter, then he really had the gift of the gab. In fact, it was probably him trying to sell you that dodgy double-glazing!

Apart from seeing those wonderful Herefords on Ulupna Island cattle stud, the highlight of my trip was when

Ron casually announced that, after a few profitable days of hard-sell, he fancied a bit of R&R on the beach. I was scheduled to fly home that next day but he persuaded me that a few days on the Gold Coast would do me good, and he was paying. Hmm, let me think….

A couple of flights later, accompanied partway by the aforementioned horse, and there we were in a 19th floor hotel suite, overlooking a beach called Surfers Paradise. It took quite some courage to phone the trouble-and-strife back home to break the news that I would be away for an extra 5 days, with the phone two feet away from my ear. I tried to tone it down by saying we were looking at some heifers.

And we were - thousands of impossibly good-looking two-legged ones!

It was here where I realised that, if all else went wrong in my world, I could always return and take up my vocation in life.

For on the entrance to that white-sandy beach was a little old guy - he must have been 110 if he was a day - with a rusty old air-compressor. For two dimes, he would fire up the machine and spray you all-over with coconut oil, front and back. And all day long, he had a queue of heavenly bodies awaiting their turn.

Now that, my dear friends, has to be the greatest job in the world.

Chapter 10 – The Loose Moose

Charlie, I apologise once more that this book is becoming a bit of a jumble, especially the last couple of chapters, which are back to front. Maybe I will rearrange them before it gets to you, but if not, try and stay with it. Please?

Back in the land of reality, my little business was flourishing but the supplies I had been bringing in from across the Atlantic had been sporadic at best. It was time to find a new supplier.

Rather than go alone, in a bid to retain friendship with my blonde mate, Pete – he who was humiliated on National Welsh TV – I invited him along. Now Pete didn't have a lot of money – nor did I to be fair – and questioned the cost.

No problem, said I, we'll sleep with cows.

That set him at ease. He had been a little apprehensive because Pete's only other trip abroad until that date had been to the Isle of Wight. The thought of having some bovine company on his journey tipped the balance and counted him in.

Three weeks later we rolled up, complete with sleeping bags, at the Toronto Winter Fair - a massive gathering of animals, once again in the centre of a city. Bold as brass, the pair of us marched into the stockmen's quarters, announced ourselves as two steer-jockey's from England, and could someone please find us each a bed.

That they did.

Not the most comfortable one, to be honest, and it might have been better if it had a mattress, but a place to sleep nonetheless, for a whole week – buckshee.

As it was evening, we threw in our two penneth towards a party that was about to ensue. Timing is everything.

Charlie, have you ever been to a drive-in off-license in a massive pick-up truck?

I have.

'Fill her up, boys..' said our driver, handing over a large wad of 100 dollar bills. I kid you not, they loaded a pallet of Coors on the front, one of Molsen on the back and yet another on top of that until the springs went down to near ground level. Then enough spirits to blow-up the Houses of Parliament on the roof of the cab, and back we went.

No soft drinks - those were for poofs.

Why cattlemen are such alcoholics, I have no idea. But, thankfully it's a global thing, not just us Brits.

Good.

It's rude to drink alone.

With the party at full swing, at about 10pm someone shouted out above the hullabaloo: Tie Out Time!

What was that?

TIE OUT TIME!

Before I could question it a third time, these three words emptied that party faster than a fart in a phone-box. Intrigued, Pete and I followed the mass exodus as 100 stockmen headed for their animals like the start of a 1950's grand prix.

'Here, hold this….and this, and this…..oh, and this.'

Not one, but 4 ropes were thrust into my hand and the same again to my mate. On the end of those ropes were 4 huge docile animals, as we followed the queue, to the main exit.

Now bear in mind that Toronto Exhibition Halls are bang in the middle of the city, surrounded by possibly the busiest road network on the Northern American continent. Quite fortunately, as it happens, as 25 metres above us was the main highway flyover. With one farmer stopping the traffic on the main road that passed the door, 500 cattle were led from the building, out into the freezing cold night, and tied to railings which had been erected directly underneath the flyover.

Basically, for these animals that had been born and bred on some of the coldest farms on earth, it would be far too warm inside a massive concrete building overnight. Sleeping out in minus five was a much healthier option, despite it being in a city centre.

To make sure that the local yardies didn't sneak up and help themselves to some prime beef during the hours of darkness, a pair of stockman, with a tin of Molsen in one hand and a Winchester under-loader in the other, were positioned one at either end of the tie-out until daylight came up, while the rest of us headed back inside and cracked open another tinny.

How bizarre!

Next day, after a couple of meetings that I had gone there to conduct, and then a few hours watching the judging of more stick-insects, Pete and I decided to go and see what down-town Toronto had to offer.

Jumping off the local rail network, a bar loomed in front of us by the name of the Loose Moose.

Perfect.

My turn to get em lined up, while Pete popped off to use the toilet.

No, not the drinks – the mooses….

By the time he came back, there were 4 drinks on the bar, and two local birds sitting attentively while being chatted up by yours truly. Now, being a married-man, I was contented with having conversation and some mild flirting with the slightly older and somewhat uglier one, leaving the stunner for my 'bachelor' mate – as you do. Well, I did still owe him one after ridiculing him in front of 5 million viewers.

Next morning, Pete arrived back at the exhibition hall looking slightly green as he divulged that his conquest owned a water-bed and he had been riding the ocean waves all night!

Still - better than a bed with no mattress at all.

Chapter T – for Texas

The upshot of the trip to Toronto was that, as far as business was concerned, it had been a complete waste of time.

It transpired that nearly all the grooming products in Canada had themselves actually been imported, from USA.

Doh!

Oh well. Better make another trip then, eh?

Next time - down to the cowboy country.

Leaving my wife at home with a two year-old, this time I boarded a jumbo bound for Houston with another mate – the aforementioned Mark Lewis.

Unlike Pete, whose previous exploits outside the UK's shores had been non existent, Mark had travelled extensively. On leaving school he had packed up his sheep-shearing equipment, gone south and done two tours of New Zealand, long before I met him. He was/is the finest dresser of show-sheep I had/have ever known. We were a good team and worked together frequently preparing cattle/sheep for sales, him teaching me the ways of the hand-shear – for sheep – and me him about clipping cattle. Often these jobs had been quite lucrative.

For you, Charlie – the term 'dressing' stock actually means undressing them; like, uh, clipping them into shape, a la paragraphs previous. Not putting them in women's clothing.

But both of us were aware that the real groomers were the yanks. Well, it's common knowledge that they do everything to extremes, isn't it?

The Texas Livestock Show and Rodeo was no exception.

After a 2 hour excursion around Houston's 6 lane ring-roads at 3am - being hopelessly lost – which included an almost suicidal 80 mph drive down the wrong side of the freeway, we eventually dropped into a late-night café, for breakfast.

Charlie, have you ever seen two white-suited Mexican bandits drag somebody outside at gunpoint?

I have.

Bang!

Screech of tyres.

The whole operation.

We would have called the police but a) they might have shot us too if we tried and b) I am not totally convinced that they might actually have been the police. Well, I have seen a few episodes of Miami Vice.

Welcome to Texas – have a nice day!

We left quietly by the back door, eventually getting to our beds in a dingy motel that I'd booked, shortly before dawn.

As with my trip to Canada, I had set up a meeting with a supplier of all things cattle showing, this time with a man by the name of John Patterson. By now I had already placed and received one big order from him, something in excess of five grand's worth and, because of this, somehow I guessed he might be pleased to see me.

After waiting an hour, eventually we sat down to discuss regular orders – paid in advance – as well as logistics, labelling and a few other details.

You know when some times in your life you instantly decide you don't like somebody? Well, this happened to me within minutes of meeting Mr Patterson. He was rude, obnoxious, awkward and generally horrible.

And he treated me with such scorn, you would have thought I had run over his cat.

Well here I was, just about settle into a contract worth £15-20,000 per year with the miserable git - and it didn't quite feel right.

Housed in Houston's massive Agri-dome, the Texas Livestock Show sprawled on from one hall to another, each one brimming with more and more breeds of cattle, many of which I had never heard of before, let alone seen. In all there were in excess of 5,000 animals exhibited over a period of 2 weeks – something that makes our own Royal Shows look like a garden fete. As it happens, in another hall we stumbled across a second purveyor of grooming equipment, an outfit I was unaware of, despite my research, that went by the name of Hamms Supply Co. Their smart exhibition stand was fronted by a jovial chap called Jim Watson whom – it was fairly obvious by the trade they were doing – everyone seemed to like. Within minutes of our introduction, unlike the man I had just walked away from, this chap invited us in, gave us a drink or two and generally made us feel at ease. With his bushy sideburns and southern drawl, as punters came to his stall, he would introduce us as if we were his best friends – all the way from lid'l old England.

Before I knew it, Jim had made a phone call to Mr Hamm himself, now a wealthy old man, and we had chatted about my requirements. By that evening, a deal had been struck worth a considerable sum - leaving Patterson well out in the cold.

Somewhere in the midst of this tale, there is a highly valuable lesson to be learned.

And here comes another one – or two.

That very same evening, Jim had been instructed by his

In Bed With Cows

boss to *'take these limey boys out and show them a good time!'*

He did try, bless him, I'll give him that. But very soon, the pointy-toed boot was very much on the other foot, as it was us showing him how to party, albeit at his boss's expense.

The first lesson he had, was how to drink whisky. Away with those tall glasses, with a shot of bourbon in the bottom, barely enough to stain the glass, topped up with lemonade and ice.

In England, well Scotland to be precise, we drink proper Scotch whisky – in tumblers - straight. Poor Jim didn't stand a chance and by the fourth round, we left him sitting in a bar somewhere with a dazed grin on his face as we headed off elsewhere for more excitement.

Well, it was Mark following the excitement, to be honest, with me tagging along behind. For the excitement he was after – to use a cattle-term here – had a great tail-end that waggled seductively, even when she was standing still.

Even with my limited experience, from my standpoint this one had a big sign above her head which said: DANGER. Strangely enough, my pal couldn't see that – all he could see was one saying SEX.

I never did establish what this girl's name was, but she was affectionately referred to by all the other lads as '19'.

And, she was unattached.

Now, I have to say, she did look at least 19 but you can never be too sure of self-appointed nicknames.

One thing she definitely was, though, was extremely hard-to-get. That had been pointed out to us - well to me anyway, Mark wasn't listening - by a few of the lads with her.

For the next while, I watched my pal, who was both younger and far better looking than I, chase 19 round the dance-floor with his tail in his hand. The more she gave him the heave-ho, the more he tried, and the more I sniggered.

Ha.

But then, I found the real reason why 19 was called 19 - which had nothing to do with her age at all, although she was actually only 18.

It was the fact that she was an only child and her father, bearing in mind this *IS* Texas, owned 19 oil-wells!

No wonder the boys were chasing her? On receipt of that little gem I considered joining the dance. But then my source confirmed that the reason her Dad had so much oil was that he, as with his family before him, were the meanest, nastiest sons-of-god-damned-bitches in the whole damn state.

Furthermore, any boy, let alone a Limey – well technically a Welshman, to be precise – caught within so much as a sniff of her snuffer was liable to meet the wrath of the huge old-man and his extra-huge fists before daybreak - or rib-break, arm-break and leg-break, to be more accurate.

By the time I managed to catch up with him to proffer the sort of advice that one feels one's buddy should hear to avoid him being found wearing a concrete waistcoat with lead buttons, face down in Houston harbour, he was actually doing rather well and had managed to buy her a drink. On receiving information that maybe it should be her doing the buying as she could afford to buy us all one, as well as the bar we were in - and probably the whole bloody block - out of her small-change, he still didn't get the message.

Eventually, I left him to it, bidding him farewell with a promise that I would mail his mother when I got back to UK, denying any part in his dismissal from this planet. Meanwhile, I had hooked up with a bunch of party-goers and we headed off to see Huey Lewis and the News who was playing next door. He was brilliant too.

In Bed With Cows

And then, to the final act of the night, well as far as I was concerned, I couldn't speak for my poor drowning buddy, the Grande Finale.

Garth Brooks.

Who?

You know him? Garth Brooks, the world's largest selling artiste of all time, that's who.

Country music is not my favoured genre and I have to say that he was bloody dreadful.

I left after the first number.

On my way out, I met my pal coming in, his hair ruffled and a glint in his eye. It was definitely time to leave.

For both of us.

Fast.

As luck happens, a bunch of guys and girls we had met earlier were heading in the same direction as our motel, and we hitched a ride in their pick-up truck. Although a bit crowded in the front, I managed to jump up on the engine cowling and was chatting to the driver about this and that during our short 20 minute journey.

But then, a couple of times I noticed that he was changing gear, using my knee. You tend to notice things like that, no matter how drunk you are.

But this was Texas! Men's Country.

And a lot of years before that film **Broke Back Mountain**.

Still, I did think it rather odd.

On arrival at our motel, the two girls stripped off and dived in the swimming pool and, naturally, I joined them.

What?

Oh, come on, it was summer….

….and I was a million miles from home….

…and slightly drunk.

Although Mark didn't join in, he did watch from the sidelines and I could hear him sniggering somewhere in the distance. Meanwhile, in the not so distance, like, er, right there behind me, wherever I managed to swim to, was our driver, grinning seductively.

Distressing though I found this, I did manage to twig eventually and escape his clutches, you will be delirious to know. Running for the sanctuary of my motel room with my manhood hanging in shame, I passed my mate who was now laughing his socks off. It transpired that on our journey back, the girls had warned Mark that this guy batted for the other side and had suggested that he was possibly quite keen on me. They even warned him that I should be careful.

But then Mark thought it would great fun, not to bollocking-well tell me….!

Bastard!

Especially after how I had tried to aid him earlier and save him from an appointment with heavy bruising!

Friends like that? I could manage without, thank you. I was quite hurt, you can imagine.

It all ended hunky-dory in the end though, as it also transpired that *both* the girls fancied me too – and *not* my film-star-like pal.

Well, that's my story anyway, and I'm sticking to it.

The whole rodeo was a huge spectacle, though, and during those few days we witnessed the world finals of brave cowboys attempting to ride bulls weighing over a ton in the name of entertainment. What a nutcase sport that is? It certainly wasn't for me. I was definitely on the side of the beasts and willing each and every one of those Stetsons to get trampled on.

There was also steer wrestling - something for which I almost felt qualified - as well as calf tying, where an animal was let loose in the ring and then a cowboy was timed how fast he could run after it and tie it up with a rope so it couldn't move. The world record for doing this is an astonishing 6 seconds! Now there's a talent we could all use, even if it's just to make a citizens arrest. Sure would have come in handy at the Royal Show.

But the one I got by far the most enjoyment out of watching was the Cutting Horses, a more skilful event I don't think there is on this Earth.

Charlie, I am not sure if you know what a cutting horse is?

Maybe our stockperson doesn't either? Let me explain.

Don't worry, it doesn't have anything to do with chainsaws, or knives.

No horses were harmed in the making of this book!

In the western states of America, Horses have been used to herd and drive cattle for nearly two centuries. As with most occupations with origins in the past – such as *'throwing the hammer'* which originated when a blacksmith once hit his finger – or the *discus* which was the Greek's way of avoiding washing up – so the skills of man and horse versus cow likewise evolved.

Now, despite me writing a whole book about my affections with the cattle species, it has to be said they are not the cleverest of animals. Basically, when it boils down to it, they run on instinct, usually en-mass.

The object of Cutting is for a cowboy and his horse to break up a bunch of cattle, and then using a series of rapid turns that would even unseat Frankie Dettori, the horse prevents one cow from returning back to its herd for as long as possible. When I say, THE HORSE, I mean just that, as the rider is allowed no say in the matter. He just sits there, holding on for grim death as these magnificent creatures bow and weave at the most impossible angles, defying the laws of nature – and physics – in the most majestic fashion.

I probably didn't explain that very well, but suffice to say, it is one of the most incredible spectacles I have ever witnessed and probably the only type of horse to which I would give the time of day.

OK – that's upset Charlie now, I am sure she adores horses.

Sorry.

But, in general, I don't!

I have my reasons.

Chapter 12 – Perth

No, we're not back in OZ again, that's enough with the globe-trotting stories for now. In fact, as I write, I never have been back to Australia although I have followed a couple of rugby tours around New Zealand.

This Perth, as any beef cattle person will tell you, is the home of the bull.

A whole load of bull.

It is in Scotland, somewhere between Edinburgh and Inverness. Originally built as a spa-town, its city centre offers some splendid architecture jumbled up with a few seventies monstrosities.

I have to say, it is one of my most favourite cities – on Earth.

Only once did I get to the old market before they tore it down to build a Willie Lowe's supermarket, losing one of the cattle-world's oldest and most famous monuments in the process. But to a beef-cattle enthusiast, it was magical. With all the byres built predominantly of wood, every scar and splinter from years of housing thousands of bulls gave it immense character. In its centre, a wooden spiral ramp supported on Victorian steel pillars curled its way up to the second floor – yes a cattle market on two floors, unheard of today.

The year I went there I had 3 Simmental bulls to prepare for sale, two owned by a nice lady – if not somewhat neurotic - from Cheshire and one from a miserly old man named Arthur Parker. Now Arthur was perhaps the meanest man in the world - meaner than Shylock himself - and for that very reason his bull was quite thin. Arthur has not been a great breeder, as he could never quite bring himself around to laying out decent enough money for a stock bull. But one day, a couple of years before I arrived, his herd had been put on the map. For he had sold a young bull at Perth for just over the upset price – in those days 1000 guineas – to a recognised and respected breeder and he, in turn, had fed the poor thing the ration it deserved. A year later, Milson Matchmaker turned up at the Royal Show in his best clothes and won the overall championship.

Charlie, let me just fill in a few basics of selling pedigree bulls in simple terms. Whereas events such as Smithfield were more of a sort of sporting occasion, pedigree bull sales were – and are - the business end of cattle breeding. Young bulls are selected from the herd and fed extra rations, then paraded against others of the same breed at a pre-sale show before being sold to other cattle breeders. Most of these animals will find their way onto farms which keep commercial cows, siring calves that will eventually end up slaughtered for beef.

The very good ones, however, will be bought by other pedigree breeders and used in the herd as a stock sire. This outcome is every breeder's goal, to sell their bulls to other breeders.

Of the very good ones, only a tiny percent are good enough to end up at the pinnacle of all bull sales, Perth. Sadly, even though some are considered by their proprietor to be good enough for this event, their sights are often not set high enough. To maintain an extra-special standard of quality, an <u>upset price</u> – the lowest price an animal can be sold for at that event – is imposed, and if an animal doesn't reach that price, it remains unsold. Often on these occasions, a well-meaning butcher will be hovering around and will take the creature off the owner's hands at meat price.

There, did that make any sense? Probably not?

Let's just say that, by breeders standards, Arthur's bulls were not normally quite on the money. That, I found out, when I arrived.

What I also found out was: nor was he.

After putting his bull through the ring and getting it

sold for a commendable 1750 guineas, I suggested that now was a good time to pay my fee, which was at that time, £100 per head. For this, the animal had been washed everyday, blown dry, clipped, groomed, shown and presented to auction. Arthur considered this to be a little on the high side, and offered me a tenner! Bear in mind I had travelled 500 miles to the sale, stayed in a hotel for 5 nights and drunk a few gallons of beer, as well as fed myself, I mused that this was a tad unfair. Furthermore, I pointed out that had it not been for the excellent way in which his bull had been presented, it probably wouldn't have sold at all. But the tenner still stood. Needless to say, I never worked for that man again. You live and learn.

Ironically, after Arthur's widow passed away a few years ago, his Shropshire farm came up for let and my old pal Mark and his wife Helen now farm it. Having spent 10 years farming in North East England growing their solid Redhill herd of Limousin cattle, this was something of a coincidence to say the least.

That same year I was there, the standard of Charolais bulls mesmerised me and I vividly remember watching with awe as Maerdy Director from Welsh vet and genius Esmor Evans broke the breed record at 56,000gns, under the experienced hammer of that wily auctioneer, the late Jack Young. A record that stood for 22 years.

However, any of the older cattlemen reading this will inform you that the real heyday for Perth auction mart was back in the late 1960's when the Argentineans came to play.

Long before Maggie and Galtieri got to falling out over some worthless islands full of sheep in the South Pacific, Argentina became a super-power in feeding the world, and specifically the WW2 troops, with Corned Beef.

So it was that Senor Bentos and his buddies journeyed half across the globe to this small town in Scotland to find their bloodstock.

Unlike in this day of Simmental, Charolais, Limousin and the like, back then there were only two main breeds, the afore-mentioned Aberdeen Angus and the Beef Shorthorn.

Famous herds such as Newhouse of Glamis, Eastfield – from a certain Tom Brewis, he in the Australian story – and Candacraig became household names as they regularly flogged bulls for five figure sums. Can you imagine the stir when, in 1963 a bull sold for 60,000 guineas?

Sixty grand is a still a heap of cash today, but back then, when land was valued at a few quid per acre and houses cost tuppence, this really was a king's ransom. For the price of one bull you could have bought the entire town of Perth – or Wales.

One thing was for sure – like all good things, it was never going to last. By the time I got into the business, the Angus breed was struggling in the same way that the Hereford did. That is until one day, about 15 years ago, a few enthusiasts, with the late George Cormack at the spearhead, managed to enlighten the world with the fact that Aberdeen Angus beef tastes better than any other.

They may well be right.

Almost overnight the Angus became a brand and a household word, as Aberdeen Angus steakhouses sprung up in every town across the country. In fact, I recall George winning the Royal Show with a bull called Mr. Steakhouse. A trifle harsh, I think. Poor thing lumbering around the ring, dwarfing George, advocating to folks everywhere that pretty soon it, and all its siblings, were destined for the dinner plate can't have been much fun.

Anyway, enough of the history lesson. Our cattleman/woman/person has probably left now, shut the cover and gone to the pub. Either that or died of boredom.

Where were we? Oh yes…

Apart from witnessing some of the world's best cattle, my twice annual trip to Perth – a week in early Feb and another in mid October - became the highlight of my year - purely because we had such a laugh.

Having already tagged the cattleman as an incurable alcoholic, you can imagine that the centre of a gathering such as this was, although not so much nowadays, the market bar. At the old mart, this constituted a fall through the door to the commercial bar of the Waverley hotel next door. However, after its demise, the new market ended up out on the bypass, a twenty minute taxi ride from civilisation which did fragment some of the night sessions, admittedly. None-the-less, in the market bar at Perth, jokes were recited, pranks were played as well as the odd business deal struck.

As with the summer shows, with my sales head on, I would duck and dive amongst the cattlemen, casually dropping my hottest product into the conversation along side the latest story I had to tell. In fact, despite having a trade-stand in the main concourse, I was more often to be found in the bar, especially in late afternoon, where I would do far more business.

I announced at the start of this book that the chronology may not be ordered correctly so I make no apologies now for digressing off on a slight tangent for a page or so. I'll do my best to tie it back in again shortly after I make this statement:

I don't particularly like South Africans.

There, that's just lost a few thousand readers, eh?

But I do have a specific and, I feel, justified reason.

In 1987 I received a phone call, out of the blue, from a man of the aforementioned origin with a thick boorish accent. Always open to opportunities, I listened intensely to what he had to say – and to sell.

The man's name was Lawrence Potgeiter and he had discovered on his travels a new style of animal clipper which had just been developed in California. With himself more interested in the horse market, he suggested that I may want to come into partnership with him, using my contacts to market it to the cattle trade. I will admit he was a persuasive chap, with patter as slick as the beautifully streamlined product he was marketing. And it was a *great* product.

Very soon he took me in.

….very soon I made one of the biggest mistakes of my life.

Together, we formed a company called Shear-Ease. Quite a catchy name, huh? How ironic then, that it was with such sheer ease I let the biggest conman since Nick Leason walk into my life and whip the rug from under me.

Completely my fault, I am the first to admit. I have never been a person to attribute blame to others. But in certain extreme cases, I do believe in revenge.

Lawrence, dear chap, if you ever get to read this, I do hope you are still looking over your shoulder?

Anyway, without boring you rigid with details, the company ran for 6 months before he buggered off with all my loot.

Ahem. Will you excuse me if I just take a short walk to calm the rage that still burns inside me some 25 years later….

….thanks. That's better.

Prior to that memorable event, sales of this smart cordless clipper went viral. Everyone wanted one. OK, it wasn't quite like an i-pod/pad, but to a cattle groomer it really was the business – that is until it went wrong.

For us, with a retail price of over two hundred quid, it was also highly profitable.

OK, back to Perth.

In a bid to display this new gadget at every available opportunity, I used to keep one in my pocket and show it to any prospective customer, even in the bar. Aha. At last we're getting to the point.

Cordless cattle clipper? Drink? You know what's coming, don't you?

At that time a very large rugby player – possibly one of the best and meanest flankers to ever pull on the Scotland jersey – was a regular at Perth as his family had an excellent herd of Charolais cattle. Let's just call him JJ.

'Frazier, ya wee English bastard,' growled this beast of a man to I, menacingly enough that I nearly kacked myself. 'Gimme a look at those clippers.'

A giant gnarled hand stretched in my direction.

'Do they cut?' questioned the great fellow, known to many, for obvious reasons, as the White Shark.

Seeing not only a prospective sale but also the chance of a household name endorsing my product, I launched into my sales patter and was in mid-flow when JJ decided to test them himself – on his mate.

Poor Pinky never stood a chance as, with athletic ease, the big man trapped him in a headlock that would have held a crocodile. Thankfully for me, although not for Pinky, three very impressive swathes over the top of his head left him with a bald patch like Friar Tuck.

'Eye, neh bad…' he grinned.

He never did buy a set though. But plenty of other folks did after witnessing that incident.

The trips to Perth continued for the next 15 years or so but I won't jump the gun just yet. Be patient.

I may just recall a couple of other escapades that we got involved in at Perth, though, if you don't mind. Over the next year or so, my life changed dramatically - the details of which I will save for another chapter.

But, basically, I gained a new partner in crime and a life-long close friend to boot. His name was also Mark. And we would work side by side for the next 4 years.

Already an established public speaker, Mark had an unsurpassed sense of humour. His comedy timing was as impeccable as Groucho Marx and the contents of his stories better polished than the World Cup. Mark's humour also dovetailed perfectly into mine in a manner that no one else has ever done. We were a double act, with the ability to bounce stories off each other that would bring guffaws of laughter from all around.

If I were inclined, I could probably fill the remainder of this book and half of the next one with tales of the shenanigans that we got up to at Perth.

Strangely enough one of them involved a nightclub *called* Shenanigans. One night, lured by the sounds of the Bay City Rollers piping out from its doorway as we passed, we were then refused entry by a behemoth with a neck like a birthday cake, only with less intelligence.

'Are you a member?' it says.

'Yes, I'm a Country member…' replies I.

'Oh yes, I remember,' quips Mark.

Think about it…..

Oh, please yourself.

That same night – I can never quite remember what I

had done wrong – I found myself on the wrong end of a kangaroo court in the lounge of the Waverley Hotel.

Charlie, if you are not sure what one of these is, ask a rugby player who has been on tour and missed a vital tackle.

With Mark as the judge and a rather biased jury including a very young Sally Crowe and Lynn Gunn, I was declared guilty - before the charge had even been read out. My defence lawyer, Harvey Atkinson, even agreed that my evidence was thinner than a Holstein cow, and I was duly sentenced – to a roll in the deep snow outside, minus my troosers! Sally, if that photo is for sale, I will gladly give the proceeds of this book to have it destroyed along with the negs!

For some strange reason, on another night we were in an Indian restaurant quite late when one of the clients started playing the piano. Where the joint was and why it had a piano in situ I haven't the faintest idea but, not being ones to resist a jaunty sing-along, we dutifully joined in.

As the evening drew to a close, its grand finale was Harry Belafonte's The Banana Boat Song. You know the one?

'Day-o…ezay-day-ay-o!'

'Daylight come and we wanna go home…'

One guy – a complete stranger to us – was giving the old: '***DAY***-O!' at the top of his voice, and then 3 of us would join in with the chorus.

Now I'm not sure if you remember the Stan Freberg version of this song? Where the bongo player says: 'It's too loud man, you're singing right in my ear.' A classic.

Well Mark instigated this version – and sent him outside into the street. Fair dos to the bloke, he did give it everything and even through a closed door we could still hear him.

'Still too loud, Man. Go further back…'

Half way down the street, he gave it an even louder go: DAAAAAYYYYY-O!!!

Again we joined in.

'Still too loud, Man..' Mark had to yell this as he was now 200 yards away.

Off he went, right to the very end, 500 yards this time. Bearing in mind, it was after midnight – and pitch dark – we could barely see him at all. But we could hear him, as could probably every sleeping resident in Perthshire.

With one final hoorah, he gunned it again:

DAAAAAAAYYYYYYYYYYYYYAAAAAYYYY-O!! EZAY-DAAYYAA-O!

The last we saw of him, was him being arrested by two bobbies, as he desperately protested that he just having a friendly sing-song with his buddies.

'There they are, look,' we could imagine him saying, pointing into the pitch blackness as they carted him away.

You had to be there...

Chapter of Change

Having ploughed a considerable sum of money into the partnership with my South African friend - which was all blown on marketing, including funding a trip for him to go and visit the manufacturers in San Diego - as well as over-trading in my own business, things were starting to get a little tight with the Bank.

In a bid to consolidate both enterprises, I laid off my two full time staff – the very able Jackie who handled phones and accounts, and Lisa who looked after packaging and mail-order - and built an office, again at my expense, on his small farm on the island of Anglesey in North Wales.

I would travel to the shows, looking after the sales side of things and Lawrence, along with his charming and long-suffering wife would handle all the stock, and despatch orders. It seemed a good solution, although I was a little dubious that all my stuff was now 200 miles from home.

Business did thrive for a while but never smoothly. Lawrence struggled to handle the orders with any efficiency and also had his mind on other things, so we employed a local guy to run the office for us, lifting a lot of it out of my control.

With the bank overdrawn and stock-levels well out of kilter, I then got a phone call, right out of the blue, from Lawrence saying he was 'pulling out', leaving me high and very, very dry. And there was absolutely bugger-all I could do about it.

From where I stood, the future days looked as bleak as a mountain blizzard – in only your underwear. And the nights were no longer providing sleep.

Thankfully, a few years earlier, I had started a crop-spraying business which just about propped up our outgoings, as well as filling in with a few tractor driving jobs to make up.

However, as sometimes happens in life, fate was just arriving round a blind bend ahead.

While staring dejectedly at a pile of invoices, many of which were at 60 days plus, I received another phone call out of the blue, this time from one of my suppliers – a company called Ritchey Tagg.

After a few discussions and a night out with the MD, a deal was struck where not only would they buy my company for a very reasonable sum but also they wanted me as part of the package.

For the first time in my life - and only time, to date - I was employed.

Bank account back in the black, company car, expense account, salary and bonuses were, in my mind, only a small part of the deal. To me, the best bit of all was that I would get to carry on doing what I loved the most, this time getting paid for it – going to cattle shows.

Although based from home, for the next four years I got to travel the UK and some of Europe organising, running and manning a high quality exhibition unit selling excellent merchandise to people I already knew. It was like taking sticky ice-cream from a sleeping baby – and I loved it.

For my very first trip, I took a ride with my new boss, a vibrant if not sometimes egotistical female by the name of Kim, to one of the best cattle shows on Earth, the Black Isle show. On a sunny August day, my birthday, as it happens, I announced to all and sundry that from now on all my range of products would be available through Ritchey's national network of distributors and here was my new business card – Andy Frazier, Retail Manager.

In Bed With Cows

Fraz was back in the game.

Strutting around that event, dazzling Kim with not only my impressive list of contacts but my ever growing knowledge of livestock in general, after months of brain-diminishing headache, was akin to an escape from Alcatraz.

With her at my side, I can vaguely remember standing on my hotel balcony, gazing at the magnificent sunset that evening believing that a light was shining down on me, giving me a second chance.

Needless to say, I had just had too much malt whisky. It does that to you…

Right, that's enough of the romantic slushy stuff, let's get back to some cows again.

Where shall we go now?

I know, how about Smithfield?

Don't groan, please. There won't be more boring anecdotes about Welshmen in underground bunkers; this time it will be a lot more upbeat, I promise.

Having said that, it will feature the Welsh again.

So let's do another chapter.

You can even have a sleep in the meantime.

Andy Frazier

Chapter 137 – well it seems like it

My first appointment as a cattle judge was handed to me when I was just 19 and from then on, my experience evolved me to a reasonably competent level.

That initial engagement in itself was no mean feat, judging the butcher's cattle at the little known but legendary Llannafen Show, near Builth Wells. Those who have been there refer to this overgrown garden fete as a 3 day show, as it takes a day to find it, a day to exhibit and a day to get over it!

From then on I had a few annual appointments, many of which were again in Wales, as well as ones in Middle and North England.

In the mid eighties I had won Birmingham Fatstock Show with a steer owned by John Bliss and his father Eric, who were butchers from Suffolk. It probably wasn't my greatest victory and, as I think John would agree, maybe not the worthiest winner on the day. But it was a win all the same, and the product of my own fair and steady hands. A year later, I helped Doug Lloyd to the championship of the very first Welsh Winter Fair, with a superb Charolais steer that sold for a whopping £7000.

Steadily my reputation as a coiffure was growing and demand for my hair-dressing skills escalated.

From then on, for a good few years, before I joined the heady ranks of employment, I would spend the winter months of November and December touring farms clipping cattle for winter fatstock shows.

This constituted me leaving home on a Monday at sparrowfart oclock, driving 5 million miles around unmarked country lanes, getting mauled by border collies and kicked

In Bed With Cows

half to death by violent untrained cattle, many of which carried no more meat than a butcher's pencil. Eventually I would arrive home for a change of clothes and some bandages at the end of the week, rest for 24 hours before starting the cycle again.

No matter, it was work and brought in cash, and I did get fed some excellent farmhouse meals en route. Often, whosever farm I finished up on for the evening would feed and board me, usually in a spare-room full of cobwebs in the attic where small children would giggle at me through keyholes. Admittedly, the odd one would have a daughter nearer my age but generally she would, quite rightly, be under lock and key.

Already growing a stronghold of clients in Wales, after my win at 'The Fair', I found myself for weeks on end travelling to places with unpronounceable names in mid-winter blizzards. On one farm, I vividly remember being tucked away in a dark shed and asking if it was snowing outside.

'Nor, just a bit of cloud, see, don't you know…'

Being one never to doubt an honest answer, when I finished the animals at 6pm, I went to open the door, only to find it was wedged shut with an 8 foot snow drift. That's how keen these people were to get their beasts clipped by the new Vidal Sassoon – as I was now named.

Not a problem, Farmer Griffiths dug me out from the drift and towed me down to the road, sending me on my way. That night it took me 9 hours to get 20 miles nearer to home when I eventually gave up when the drifts were twice to height of my van, and took refuge in a farmhouse near Bishops Castle.

At one event I had been judging during the summer, I bumped into a chap called Mr Jones who asked me if I could fit in his team of nine cattle during my November trip.

Without much more thought, his name was pencilled in the diary.

Charlie, can you imagine how Simon Cowell must feel when he discovers someone on his show with genuine talent, a diamond in the rough. Maybe a little twinge happens, downstairs? I am pretty convinced that's what drives him to continually keep making new series of his ghastly show - besides the money that is.

Or when an English teacher discovers a child who is a literary genius – or a football coach uncovers the next Wayne Rooney. Within their own vocation, this is surely their quest – to find that Holy Grail.

So it was for me. With a deep knowledge of the exact shape, size, firmness and correctness of what a champion animal should possess, combined with the style and polish I could provide on the outside, I was always on the lookout for that next champion. Constable discovering that perfect countryside scene of which to paint, or Rodin finding the perfect shaped piece of bronze from which to carve a Thinking Man.

On a dark night in mid Wales, amongst a team of 9 cattle owned by Mr Jones, there it was - a steer of near perfect proportions, with dark auburn hair and oozing style, in its ragged clothes.

Does this sound bizarre? Charlie, you think maybe I am a little perverted? I can't say I blame you, really. When I see this written down – about the ecstasy that I felt when I saw this creature - it does seem a bit odd. Maybe I should seek counselling?

For the next 6 hours I trimmed up the other 8 beasts, receiving the odd kick for my troubles, and saving the best till last. This one was to go to Smithfield and warranted the very best of my efforts. It certainly got that and wow, what a beast it turned out to be.

A few weeks later, Mountain Man waltzed into London in dazzling style, turning heads like a supermodel as he went. Here was my first real shot at the Smithfield goal. For 2 more days, I toiled at getting him in his perfect clothes until Monday when he trotted into his class of 12 other hopefuls. Ably handled by Mr Jones' pretty young daughter, Mountain Man was soon pulled into first place. We were en-route.

The next day was a different kettle of beans, though. This time he had all the other first prizes to beat, many of them former champions in their own right. After some nail biting close shaves, he managed to beat all the other males in the show. Male Champion at Smithfield. Sounds pretty good?

Congratulations Fraz – well done.

But to me, that wasn't enough.

Sadly, within the next hour, the female champion was selected and then, in the dramatic head to head finale that sets Smithfield atmosphere so far apart from any other event, we fell at the last hurdle.

2 hurdles, in fact.

As both the champion female, and reserve champion female went on to take the top two honours in the show. Not for the first time in my life, I had been beaten by two ladies.

Hmmm, did I just write that? Steady on…

Although my client was over the moon, my own disappointment was immeasurable. Here I was, in the heady number 3 spot out of 400 animals, and yet I could have wept.

As it happens, afterwards there was some controversy over the breeding details of Mountain Man, and he ended up being disqualified, so perhaps his <u>not</u> winning Supreme Champion turned out to be blessing.

I'll be back, I vowed, as I packed up my tools with my tail tucked well under me.

And I would. Because, Charlie, **failure is not an option.**

Six months later, the cycle started again. This time back in Shrewsbury at the aforementioned Shropshire and West Mid Show. Another near-orgasm experience happened when I saw Cindy from 200 paces.

The year was 1993 – I know that because it was my first year with Ritchey Tagg and also because I have a picture of Cindy on the wall in my study – naked!

Cindy, owned by another Welshman - Mr Thomas - had Champion written all over her. At the time, just an 11 month old youngster with no hair, she cake-walked that event, collecting her very first championship. Having known Dai Thomas for a good few years I then set about the task of persuading him to go for gold and exhibit her against the best-of-the-best. Swim with the sharks.

Dai didn't like sharks. I'm not sure he had ever even been to London. But I convinced him eventually that this was a once in a lifetime chance.

'A man can sleep with many things in his life…' I lectured, using the best sales pitch I could muster, '..but he should never sleep with regret!' (nor another man's wife, actually, but I left that bit out!)

It did the trick.

Seven months after that, we were back – again.

This time, instead of visiting Cindy in South Wales prior to Smithfield, I took a gamble and instructed Dai on how to wash'n'groom her and then to bring her to the show, totally unclipped.

It was a huge risk to take. What if her hair was such a

In Bed With Cows

mess that I couldn't tame it in time? What if it had all fallen out? Worse still, if it had gone too curly? She was a Limousin after all...

As soon as she came down that ramp in London I was convinced it had been the right decision. Nobody even noticed Cindy as she tramped through to her stall looking like an unkempt yak, and that suited me just fine. Because I knew this was really Kate Moss in a paint-splattered boiler-suit and bobble-hat - for I had seen her naked.

While all the others headed off to the usual parties and shindigs that happen on Friday night in Earls Court district, I had a few shandies and an early night. In my dreams I saw my grandfather sitting in his armchair telling me about that silk purse all those years earlier, and that this was my chance to be the seamstress. Go out there and do it for all to see. It was a challenge to relish and I knew I was ready.

With a clear head and steady hand the next morning I quietly collected Cindy from her stall, gave her a wash and blow-dry and then set about creating a work of art. I was Michelangelo up there in a cradle under the ceiling of the Sistine chapel - or Monet setting up his water-colours out there before the sunrise.

Normally, when I set to work clipping an animal of this nature, it would take me an hour, two at the most.

This one took longer – much longer.

Lunchtime passed, then opening time, then afternoon teatime as eventually the daylight subsided outside while I clipped away, strand by strand.

Behind me a steady stream of stockmen came to have a look as Chinese whispers fluttered on the breeze, taking in the view and silently nodding their heads as my work took shape. Great men – men who had been there and done it themselves.

By the time I was through, for the very first time in my life I realised that at last, after 15 years as a cattleman, I had joined their ranks. A boy done good - a young man who had learned from the best, now ready to take them on at their own game.

The rest was down to fate and, for once, fate was happy to back me up.

On Monday we breezed through the class into first place, taking out one or two hot contenders for the title in the process. That night, Dai and I took it in turns to sleep with Cindy, propped up on a bale with one eye open, not unlike the two burly armed cowboys that protected those Canadian beasts under the motorway a few years earlier.

I will come clean here, and admit that the reason I chose the title of this book, **In Bed With Cows**, is because of that one night. In the past there had been rumours of jealous opposition sneaking up in the middle of the night and offering substances to competing animals which would upset them for the next days challenge. I wasn't taking that risk. A night without sleep would do me no harm and it was a small price to pay for a potentially huge reward.

In my novel, **The Right Colour**, for those of you who have read it, I outlined a few suspicious acts that happened after midnight amongst the cattle-lines, albeit a little tongue-in-cheek. I also described in explicit detail the fervour of what it felt like to be in that position. Although The Princess was a work of fiction, that passion was written from my very heart.

Tuesday morning arrived.

Judgement day.

In the past I had been so near, yet so far. This time I *wanted*, and I *wanted* bad.

One by one the steer sections lined up until an overall

male winner was chosen.

Then it was our turn.

Like an ant on amphetamines, I snipped, polished and pruned at that hair, containing my nerves just enough to continue to perfection. Dai watched calmly, listening to instructions that I blurted out to him, like the trainer to a prize-fighter. Keep out of the corners. Always face the judge. Set the pace. Don't slouch.

His would be the final job, to parade my work and put in the killer blow.

Into the ring he went, taking the first hurdle of beating the other heifers of the same age group to a round of applause. Back out into the parlour, more make-up, more hairspray and off you go again, this time with his ears ringing with good luck calls.

Soon we were down to the final two.

A showdown of showdowns.

Ali versus Frazier. Borg and McEnroe. Andy Murray versus – err – well, everyone, really.

One more slap on the backside and my work would be done, either way.

At the ringside, tension grew to breaking point as Mike Tucker, the gregarious commentator, built up the atmosphere. Who would be this year's supreme?

And then it came - that immortal tap that would put Cindy, Dai and I into the history books.

The supreme champion at the Royal Smithfield show, 1993.

A lifetime's ambition, completed.

A mission rewarded.

In my belief, a reward well earned.

Wow, that all got a bit emotional, didn't it?

Did it bring a tear? It did to me.

Always does.

To cap it all, the following November I received a call from a well-known cattleman from Northern Scotland. He had suffered with a slipped disc in his back and was laid up in hospital. In his shed were 4 pretty good cattle destined for Smithfield but he was unable to clip them himself. Of all the great cattlemen in the country, it was me that he wanted to do the job for him.

Two days later I was on a flight to Aberdeen and once again facing not one but two of the best animals I had ever clapped eyed on. For two days I yet again performed my magic.

This time, having won steer champion and then supreme champion in the previous two years I was to be part of another record. One only ever achieved twice in Smithfield's 200 year history.

In 1994 I groomed both the **supreme champion** – an outstanding heifer called Miss Jackie – and the **reserve champion** as well, from the same stable. The latter, to me, was possibly the better of the two, a steer purchased from Robbie Wilson - he of Suffolk and Texel sheep fame - called the Hitman.

As you can imagine, space on the wall in my study was becoming quite scarce. In fact there was little room for any more cattle champions.

Having achieved pretty much all my cattle grooming ambitions by my mid thirties, the following year I hung up my clippers and retired from the game, apart from the odd demonstration and training event. For two very small pins I would go back to it - although now the primestock cattle world has got far too money orientated. With purchase prices often in excess of five figures changing hands as too many greedy people try to buy their glory, it is no longer a sport, but a business in which only the rich can compete.

I wish them all luck – and in most cases, that is all that they need.

Instead I crossed the tracks – and became poacher turned game-keeper. However, that story can wait a while longer.

Meanwhile, let's have a rummage around for a few more tales from that era.

And shoehorn them into yet another chapter.

Chapter 138

OK, this is going to irritate you now, but I am going to step back a couple of years. Back to the days when I was still solo and dragging cows around to earn my living, because in my haste to keep you entertained I think I missed a few crackers. Especially at the now defunct Royal Show.

The Royal was always a special place, mainly because it represented the whole country. Originally a travelling event, it would rotate between a few of the Home Counties each year until it settled on a permanent site in Stoneleigh, near Coventry in the 60s. Although its nearest town was 10 miles away, the charming Kenilworth, nobody ever went there.

As an aside, a few years ago I ended up living in Kenilworth for 8 months, right next to a pub called the Virgins. Not sure why I felt obliged to mention that.

However, during the Royal Show, which went on for best part of a week, very few people went anywhere outside of the main gates because there was no real need to. As well as the quite aptly named RANK village, a conglomeration of concrete cells set on two levels to house as many stockmen as possible, a car-park full of stock lorries served for most of us as a hotel for the week. Once the remnants of the travelling cattle had been cleared out, beds, furniture, carpets and bars were erected in its place as we all took up residence in our temporary housing like refugees.

Arranged in a circle around the cattle rings, every cattle breed society had its own pub, many of which would be open *only* to their breed members during the daytime, although with so many different breeds under my charge, I was welcome in just about all of them.

In the run up to the show, I may have visited 20 others

as far away as Cornwall, Norfolk, Edinburgh and Dumfries. On leaving each one, a handshake and a 'see you at the Royal..' was the traditional goodbye.

Hence, on the evenings during that week long endurance test, we would all catch-up once more for the annual finale. Yes, the Royal Show was a global village the likes of which the UK cattle world will never see again and, unlike Smithfield, it was in mid summer – first week in July.

With teams of cattle to prepare and a tradestand to run, for me it was my busiest and most lucrative week of the year too. Up before 5am washing cattle, partying till the small hours with thousands of people I called friends, as my colleague Brian once put it, the Royal had *'Long days and short nights…!'*

In the evening many of the different breeds would hold a bbq, each one declaring that their beef was best, in a game of one-upmanship. One year, whilst chomping on a Belgian Blue steakwich, some Shorthorn breeders came by and passed derogatory comments about how we would all need our teeth sharpened to eat that stringy old stuff. Still being heavily involved with the breed I, along with Pete Bodily, decided that we should challenge these belligerent Scots to a steak-off. Paying from our own pocket, we selected two of the best steaks we had on offer and visited their bbq with two platefuls.

'Gentlemen,' I announced, huffily, 'before you diss our product, we bid that you try some…'

Accepting the challenge with a grin, they dissected our offering, tasted it and made appreciative noises. In fact they were suitably surprised by the excellent quality of the meat although they did make a point of chewing it noisily.

Smugly we departed, considering we had just scored a point for the BB's on their road to world domination.

Thirty minutes later, a couple of chaps in kilts arrived at

our gig with two silver platters held high.

'Tis only fair we returned the compliment..' said Kilt number one.

'Aye, en you'll ney need tae chow it fer quite so long…' added number two.

From that moment on, I became an advocate of the British Shorthorn, for it was the most delicious piece of beef I have ever eaten.

So much so, that if I ever go back into breeding cattle, the Shorthorn would be my animal of choice. Back then they were a breed well out of favour, possibly on the Rare Breed's list – almost liable to extinction - as Continental breeders discarded the baby-with-the-bath-water.

Not now though.

Only a few months ago I was at Perth Bull sales – now in Stirling – giving a pal a hand as he sold 6 shorthorn bulls – not all fantastic ones either – to average £6000 each. Kind at heart and yet hardy as hell, they are an animal that can survive on a winter's hill, look after their young with the fervour of a killer whale, and yet provide beef of a quality to rival the Aberdeen Angus.

Oops. More hate-mail….

Anyway, as I mentioned, when it came to working with cattle breeds I had no real preference back then. In short, I was a prostitute and would sell my services to the highest bidder. At times when I got too many cattle to handle, I would rely on my old pal John Morris to help me out. I had met John in the early eighties and we worked well together. His calm demeanour with animals was welcomed, especially when the heat of the show-ring stirred up emotions and, in general, he was pretty reliable although, he would be the first to admit, he did have a bit of a drink problem. Along with him came his wife Cath, who organised us all, and his

In Bed With Cows

daughter Laura who was a handy runner.

On one occasion we had four breeds on the go at once – no mean feat even for you, seasoned cattleperson. Try organising that lot? Limousin and Charolais, Simmental and Blondes. Just getting them to and from the ring was like a Chinese puzzle. And we had sheep there, too.

Did I mention that my father bred sheep? No? I have promised to bore you with my background and childhood, haven't I? I won't right now, though, as we are midst showing cattle. Maybe I will put it all in another book… IN BED WITH SHEEP. Now there's one for the top shelf!

OK, back to the Royal.

One of my clients was a large as life character from Derby who ran a successful haulage business. Let's just call him Les the Lorry. Recently Les had got into Limousin cattle and I had toured with him on his first season to a number of shows in his brand new smartly painted Scania, winning a prize or two and doing OK. His border collie usually came along for the ride as well. For accommodation, he towed behind it a small caravan that was fairly meagrely appointed.

Whilst sleeping in said caravan at Rutland County show – considering Rutland is the smallest county in Britain, spanning only a few hundred hectares, the show was actually a very strong one, cattle-wise – I awoke in the morning with my eyes running.

'Can you smell gas?'

'No, must be your farts…'

Derbyshire men can be a little crude sometimes.

Off I went to feed and wash the cattle while Les did his own thing. On my return I was just near enough to witness him lighting a match to put the bacon under the grill while the dog sat on the bed.

The very next thing I saw was a border collie cascading through the door followed by a ball of flame like something from a Road-runner cartoon. As I ran to the scene of the explosion collecting a bucket of water en-route, like Kurt Russell in a scene from the film, Backdraft, Les's blackened face appeared in the doorway with his eyebrows still singeing. If only I had a video camera – it could have been a Hollywood classic.

After delivering the hazardous caravan to a scrap-yard, Les then went out and purchased a new one. Well, not exactly a new one, but one that had only a single previous owner – a gypsy. Now for those of you who may be under the impression that gypsies are poor, think again. This thing was a palace on 4 wheels. Chromed from chassis to window, it included a shiny smokestack, cut glass windows and the plushest interior I have seen outside of a 5 star Hilton.

As he parked it up at the Royal, all it needed was a lurcher tied up outside, a piebald pony and a few piles of smoking tarmac to really set the scene.

But boy, was it the party house.

Before he had gotten into cattle, Les had invested considerable money in his daughter's hobby, that of show-jumping. With her natural expertise, coupled with some of the most expensive horses money could buy, she had soon found her way to the top of that game and was competing at the highest level.

Also competing at that same level were some household names, each and every one of whom were the biggest bunch of scallywags I have ever encountered. And they all turned up, most nights, in the Gypsy café, well after midnight.

I can vividly recall the great Harvey Smith – he who was famed for his two fingered salute - being an expert yodeller. Not a lot of people know that.

In Bed With Cows

But by far the funniest was a short fellow whose name I dare not mention as he has recently been on TV inspiring a nation. Let's just call him Nicky. At that time he was one the best in the country, but inside the pikey-van amidst a drunken show of bravado, a debate raged about who was the finer competitor. After emptying the well appointed drinks cabinet, Nicky and one his buddies decided that they would show us how to do *proper* show-jumping. Loading his pal on his back, he set off, in the rain as I recall, at a canter toward the low rope that separates the car park from the road and hurdled it like the Olympian that he was.

Except, on that occasion, he didn't quite get a clear-round.

Splat went the pair of them, face down into a puddle – on the road!

Allegedly, he never made it to the jumping ring at all the next day, instead spending the whole day in bed, despite being one of the grand attractions of the event.

That same year happened to coincide with the football World Cup.

Many times in this book have I indicated that the cattle world was full of great characters, most of whom liked to take a drink. One of those was a young bearded chap who took a wee bit more than most. Born into one the greatest cattle families in Perthshire, let's just call him D-Mac.

D-Mac, not unlike most of his pals, was not adverse to winding up the auld foe, the Sassenach English. To be frank, in most cases he was well within his rights to do so, especially at the Royal when the George Cross brigade were on their home turf, arrogantly calling the shots.

Back then, the Rank village had its own bar, restaurant and TV lounge. So it was that on the second evening of the event, England were playing an epic match against Cameroon in the quarter finals and the TV lounge was packed to the gunwales. The tiny room was as crowded as an underground train in rush-hour and not a seat was to be had anywhere. With the match already well into extra time, having come from 2-1 behind, Linekar was about to take a penalty that would put England into the World Cup semi final for the first time in over 20 years.

Behind them, the door opens noisily. In walks D-Mac, pushing his way through the crowd to the front of the room, carrying a folded chair above his head.

To collective absolute horror, as bold as brass he opens the chair, sets it down in front of the TV, presses a button and changes the station……

'Anyone mind if I watch Brookside…?' he questions, matter-a-factly.

How he got out of there alive, I will never know!

Apparently he did it for a bet.

Although England did make the semis, the score that evening was definitely:

Scotland *1* – England *0*.

Before we leave the Royal for good I would like to enlighten you to the work of a Frenchman called Yann Arthus-Bertrand. Yes I know it's a long name, in France you are nobody without at least 40 letters in your surname.

Yann was a cantankerous bastard when I met him, he would probably admit that himself. But many geniuses are. And he truly was one – with a camera.

Whereas my old pal Peter Picture photographed animals to capture them at their most appealing to other cattle specialist, Yan was on a mission to get pictures for his new book – Good Breeding – where it was at much about the handler as the animal itself.

Having set up a 'studio' in a large disused building not too far from the cattle lines, he befriended me to provide him with some subjects for his photographs. Why me? Well, the first thing he required was a giant hair-drier, the sort which I had been importing from USA and selling to cattle groomers. He didn't need it to dry hair though, his requirement was to blow the dust and straw off the massive hessian sheet which was a backdrop for his animals.

One by one I provided him with animals and their owners, probably a dozen cattle in all, over the course of a day. Each time he would dither about, setting up his lens and films, as the animals and handlers got restless and danced about. Always looking for the perfect photograph of any beast, I would try and stand it in the right place to show it off correctly and Yann would oblige me with this. But what I didn't realise was that it was the quirky shot he was after, and he certainly got those. The way he managed to dovetail the emotions of the handler with that of the animal in this book are nothing less than stunning.

For example, on one photo, page 278 in my copy, Pete Bodily is trying to manoeuvre one of our Belgian Blue bulls into place by pushing the stubborn creature backwards. What comes over in that picture is a wrestling match between a 10 stone man and a giant bull, to me outlining the control that we professional stockmen have over animals ten times our size.

In another shot John Morris's daughter, 10 year old Laura – our runner – is so at ease with our Simmental bull, that he just looks like her giant pet.

Of the 300 or so pictures, many of them are taken in the Paris Show, with a few more in a field in Buenos Aires and most of them are hilarious. I am not sure this book was ever a commercial success but it is well worth a look -

although the coffee table version will set you back upwards of seventy quid.

You may have heard of Yann as he went on to become famous for his ***Earth from the Air*** series, a wonderful exhibition of creative photos taken from a helicopter of every part of the globe. Also he has become a well known environmentalist.

I just checked out his website – he still isn't smiling.

Chapter 139 – Highlanders

Horny as hell…!

That was a response I once got back from an old crofter, when I asked how his cattle were. It always stuck with me.

The Highland cattle breed are a race apart from others of their species – as are some of their breeders.

For instance, Charlie, did you know that a herd of Highland cattle is not actually referred to as a herd at all, but a FOLD. Now there's a snippet of information that may come in handy in a pub quiz.

Evolving from the hillier parts of mountainous Scotland, especially from the Western Isles, these shaggy haired beasts with outstretched horns are exceptionally picturesque out in their natural environment, if you can get near enough to them. With a resilient ability to withstand the abhorrent rain and snow in their habitat, cows are mostly left to their own devices and consequently rarely handled by humans at all. Thus, when cornered into confined spaces, they have a tendency to lash out, as would, say, a Bengal tiger. However, I would never sell their temperament short because in general, once they have been handled, they are docile as the next breed.

However, very often the ones I met were somewhere in the middle, as I will come on to in a moment.

Being as the hairy-and-horny ones were always exhibited in their natural state, when I first started to purvey my grooming products their breeders were rarely customers of mine. Then, one day, a titled Lady from the Home

Counties phoned up and ordered a drier – 300 quids worth – as, despite it being 75 degrees warmer in the south of England compared to the outer Hebrides, she was concerned that when her cattle got wet, they may catch a chill. Naturally, I concurred.

At that time, although other traditional breeds were falling from favour, the endearing qualities of the Highland had catapulted them to something of a fashion accessory, especially if you owned a big fuck-off stately home. To see a fold of such beauty happily grazing in the low meadows beside your 2 mile-long chestnut lined driveway was as much of a necessity as a view of Mount Blanc from the balcony of your alpine lodge, or giant turtles basking in the ocean shallows outside your holiday villa in Mauritius. Not only that, with names like 'Ceilidh of Bottomly Manor' or 'Secret Mistress of Iniquity Hall', they also made great conversation topics at dinner parties. Basically, what was once a functional animal, serving its purpose to control the growth of heather in unreachable places, now became a new plaything for the rich and famous. But it wasn't just the British peers and celebs that wanted them either, the wealthy Germans were after them too.

On the strength of that one phone call, I had suddenly uncovered a new seam in my marketplace. With the aid of the Highland Cattle Handbook, a cheerful little publication full of pictures of scary cows standing on mountain-tops, I copied out a list of the address of every breeder with a double-barrelled name and sent them a leaflet, explaining how their new found pets may die, were they not treated to a weekly shampoo and set. It worked like a charm and very soon the orders came rolling in.

'If Lord and Lady Snodsbury had bought a hair-drier for their one cow, Bonnie Mary the 25th, then Baroness Shipswhistle-Ogilvy would want an even bigger and more powerful one for Bitzy-Isobel the 9th, thank you very much. My people will be in touch, goodbye.'

Buoyed with this new market, I decided a trip was needed to that gorgeous little town of Oban, nestling on Scotland's western shores. In an uncannily similar coincidence to my first trip to Perth, Oban's old mart had too been sold to be replaced by a supermarket, and this was to be its last sale before it was destined to be demolished.

Oban sales were, and still are, the home of the Highlander in the same way that Perth sales had been home to the Aberdeen Angus. And, purely by happenstance, I was to arrive at the biggest sale of them all.

Earlier on in this book, I mentioned the onset of BSE and the media hype that surrounded it. As it happens, by the time the following sale came around, cattle exports to Germany had been outlawed and, furthermore, owning cows as play-things was no longer trendy.

Arriving in Oban in my van laden with goodies, it was obvious there was a buzz about the place. In that cramped old market, complete with wooden railings worn thin to breaking point, stood row upon row of golden brown animals, their horns sticking up above the pens like Vikings. Talk of the Germans coming to buy had sent ripples through the moors and just about every saleable animal in Scotland had been rounded up and brought to mart. From island to island a car ferry, which had been converted to a cattle transporter for the week, docked and loaded up animals from as far away as Stornaway, Benbecula and Barra. It appeared that every crofter in the Highlands had something to sell, if the price was right.

Shuffling between the wily auld farmers in their bonnets and kilts could be found the southern gentry, draped in the finest tweed fresh from House of Bruar.

Dotted between them was the new money. One young man had made his mark in the music industry producing records for the likes of Kyle Minogue, Donna Summer and Cliff Richard. His name was Pete Waterman – as of Stock,

Aiken and Waterman – and he had, the previous year, set up a small fold of Highlanders somewhere in England. Rumours preceded him that this time around he was looking for a stock bull.

On the other side of the fence, in the blue corner, were the Germans in their trilby hats and lederhosen, accompanied by baffled translators who could no more understand the Gaelic drawl of the Highland crofters than I could.

One man, Herr Baumer, had sold his communications business in Hamburg for squillions of marks, and had already started investing heavily in British cattle. It was rumoured that he too was interested in a stock bull.

All I knew was that all these people, being worth a few quid, were potential customers. Earlier that year I had made friends with the very likeable Donald Macgillivry from the Isle of Mull, a man who knew all there was to know about the breed. Once settled into the bar, he introduced me to top breeders in rapid succession, advocating that my products were perfect for their animals. Using the great memory that I am so lucky to be blessed with, I filed away details in my head, making notes to contact them at a later date. I couldn't thank Donald enough – it was just the opening I had been after.

That night, staying in the Alexandra hotel, a place where I had stayed as a child many years before, with my father who had come for the ride along with me, I met another great man - one who would change my life.

His name was Captain J Ben Coutts.

I tell a lie, I had met Ben previously on a couple of occasions as he was involved in Smithfield show, although he would not have remembered me. Ben was meeting up with a couple of his sons, one who had travelled over from Australia and managed a huge farm over there.

In Bed With Cows

Standing at six feet six, Ben was quite a domineering man with great presence and that evening we had a superb chat. Indeed it was him who enlightened me about the little island of Kerrera, just off the bay.

'See the wee island oot there?' I squinted and nodded.

'If you can see that, it means it's going to rain…'

'Oh. Thanks for the tip.'

'Aye, and if ye cannae see it, means it's raining already!'

Little did I know that Ben and I would meet again, a year or two later, next time on foreign soil.

Back in the mart, the next day, things had hotted up to cauldron proportions. Heifers that had been, the year previous, worth £1200-1400 were now making 3-4000 as belligerent ringside bidding rivalled between the monied classes. Meanwhile, back in the bar, never had so many hands been rung in glee as overdrafts were cleared and new land-rovers ordered.

New hair-driers, too.

The highlight of the sale was a second prized bull from Donald Macgillivray, a chunky lad called Seamas 2nd of Pennygown. As previously suspected, Herr Baumer and Waterman both fancied him and the bids rattled up to £20,000 before the young whipper-snapper with the pony-tail eventually gave in to Baumer's millions.

I believe it is still the breed record to this day, and may be for many years to come.

Incidentally, I note that Pete Waterman has now gotten rid of his cattle fold, in favour of collecting steam locomotives. They probably don't kick as hard, that's for sure.

For me, this was the first of many fabulous trips to Oban although, on the next few occasions, it would be as an employee with an expense account. In fact my next trip there was a Royal affair.

Now swanning about the country in a fat company car, doing, it has to be admitted, not a great deal and getting paid for it, one of my remits was to host cattle clipping demonstrations wherever possible, under a great big Ritchey Tagg banner.

As the old mart was now demolished, with the complete wooden sale ring being bought by Herr Baumer as a souvenir, a new market had been constructed, just out of the town. Whereas the old one had been so full of character it clung to your breeks, the new one – as often happens – was as soulless as a wet weekend in Coventry.

To brighten it up, on that first event, it was decided to invite the breed's patron along to open the new mart and grab some headlines.

Her name was Anne – the Princess Royal.

The year before, as part of the Highland cattle bi-centenary celebrations - yes 200 years of hair and horns – I had been asked to clip one of these yak-like creatures for a demonstration at the Royal Highland Show for the Queen Mother. Arranged by Donald Macgillivray – he gets everywhere, doesn't he? – four suitable animals were brought over from Campbeltown on the Mull of Kintire, two of which were already clipped and two of which it was my job to de-bag – in public.

Compared to your average Charolais or Angus, clipping one these things was like trimming a leylandii hedge – with a pair of nail-scissors.

Except that a hedge generally doesn't want to kick your head off its shoulders.

Basically, these were just a couple of purebred beef animals that had been designated for slaughter. The idea of

In Bed With Cows

the exercise was to enlighten the discerning public that under all this mass of hair was beef – prime, succulent beef – that tasted every bit as good as those Aberdeen things round the corner. The fact that the 4 steers had never been handled until the week before, and then for the word handled, replace 'tied to rail and washed with a high powered steam-cleaner' had been omitted from my briefing. Now here they were on their way to the gallows, only to take a 4 day stop-over in a tent and be gawped at like some circus freaks.

Armed with a set of heavy-duty sheep shears, at 2pm each day, I attacked one animal in a gallant attempt to transform it from ear-lug to purse over the course of an hour, watched by a blood-thirsty mob who had only assembled to witness the shit getting kicked-out of me.

'Whao, steady boy...' I would mutter, going in for another swatch only to get a left hook flying past my forehead parting my hair.

It was like watching Late Night Kick-Boxing live from Vegas!

There were people with video cameras, news reporters, vegan demonstrators, St John's ambulance, clean-up contractors, even undertakers, all waiting for the car-crash like vampires at a massacre. Why I didn't wear a full-face crash helmet and body armour, I am still wondering.

Thankfully, on neither of the two occasions did the QM turn up to witness the spectacle, or else we might have made it onto national TV. In hindsight, I was damn lucky I didn't make it onto an episode of Casualty, as the bruises mounted up.

Furthermore, when I had finished, instead of now looking like prime beef, the poor wretched creatures looked like they had been run over by a Claas Lexion combine. It definitely wasn't the masterpiece I had been looking for – my Michelangelo moment of fame had turned into Michael

Badhair Williams (look him up). I certainly wasn't going to get any hedge-cutting contracts from the ordeal, either.

And so, back to Oban, the following Spring.

Still on their mission to market prime Highland beef – which I have to say *is* delicious - yet another demonstration was planned where, once again, I would shave a Highland beast and expose its nakedness to the Royal family.

Thankfully, this one was a little calmer, although it still wasn't overly keen on being undressed and even less on the flash photography burning its retinas, and I did manage to coiffure it into something resembling a smart looking steer in about 40 minutes.

All the while, Anne kept one watchful eye on me, possibly considering changing her hair-dresser. She was definitely impressed, especially when I finished and then sprayed on some hair-spray, showed it a mirror and asked it if it wanted something for the weekend…

NOT.

'You've taken away all its character…' were her first words.

'But…but…but…' muttered I, reconsidering my *by Royal Appointment* status.

'Poor thing, fancy stripping away all that hair. It just looks like an ordinary animal now…'

'Yes, that's the whole idea, you crazy woman,' were not words I was about to offer in response to this.

Instead, I found myself agreeing with her and looking around for some glue so I could stick it all back on again, for fear of ending up in the Tower.

Being the delightful human that she is, the Princess realised my embarrassment and changed the subject onto more jovial matters, enquiring as to what I did for a day job and such like, and listening intently to my stammering answers.

That, having met them both, is the difference between her and her elder brother, the fact that, even if she is not interested, she makes you feel that she is.

Her Granny was like that too – so easy to talk to, because she listened.

Charles, in my experience has a somewhat more blinkered view on red and green, and everything else is just gravy.

Oops. I've done it now, haven't I?

Insulted the Royal Family.

Should I get a lawyer? Or should I hit delete?

Maybe grow a beard and live in a cave in the Afghanistan mountains?

You'll back me up, won't you Charlie? Perhaps campaign for my release from custody, or send me a cake with a file in it?

Thanks. I knew I could rely on you.

Moving swiftly on.

I mentioned earlier in this chapter that Herr Baumer had purchased the wooden sale-ring from the old Oban market in a bid to retain some of its history. Well, he didn't just buy it for firewood, but instead re-erected the entire thing in a purposely build shed on his farm – in Hamburg. Why, I am not too sure. Because he could, I suppose.

When the BSE ban came into being, Baumer had already amassed himself with quite a few animals and, being the entrepreneur that he is, decided that now was a time to sell a few of his own, to his German buddies. Not just

German, either, but Swiss, Austrian, Danes and Norwegians. In a few years, he had become the eurohub for Highland cattle, as well as a few other breeds.

Duly a date was announced, a sale catalogue was published and a select few invitations sent out, one of which arrived on my doorstep. Along with a lot of stock from Scotland, Herr B had also taken a stockman, called Bill Smith. Prior to this engagement, Bill had managed a fold of cattle for Glasgow city council, in Pollock Park, and had also been a good customer of mine. My original invite was because he needed someone to help him groom the cattle up for sale, all 200 of them. When I replied to say that I was now gainfully employed – by Ritchey Tagg – between us we masterminded a plan along the lines of 'why not get Ritchey to set up a stand at the event to market a few of their wares'. I presented this scenario to Gordon Fabretti, our sales director, using my most persuasive tactics, and he bought it wholesomely.

Within a few weeks, I was off across Europe for the thousand mile trip towards Hamburg, in a 4x4 loaded with grooming stuff, to one of the most fabulous weekends I have ever had. Having no idea who else would be there, it was a pleasant surprise that the first person I should bump into when I pulled into the brand new cattle yard was Captain Ben himself, along with his lovely wife Sally.

'Andy, dear boy, just in time for a dram…' and off we went towards the bar – which was all free.

'Damn krauts, they're everywhere, Andy!'

It reminded me of the Major from Faulty Towers….don't mention the war.

'I don't like the krauts. Intolerable people..' he continued in a whisper loud enough to be heard in Berlin.

At the time I just laughed and it was only later, as he started telling me some most amazing tales, that I realised

In Bed With Cows

that a) he was serious and b) he had a bloody good reason not to.

Although fifty-odd years had gone by, Ben had still yet to forgive them for what they had done….

While recovering from an operation where shrapnel had removed most of Ben's nose during a battle in the Africa's Tobruk desert during World War II, he was being transported home to Blighty on a civilian ship called the Laconia when it was sunk by a German U-boat just off the Ascension Islands.

Yep, that was a far better excuse for a dislike of all things Germanic than I had for loathing anyone with blonde hair and a boorish-Dutch accent.

Over a couple more drams – my round – he recalled, with tears in his eyes, how the Laconia went down drowning over 2000 innocent people, many of them women and children. Although one of *many* initial survivors, as they drifted for 5 days, tightly packed into a tiny life-raft, quite a few others simply 'gave up the ghost' and slipped away during the night. Eventually they had been rescued by the French and taken to a POW camp in Casablanca.

As Ben would never forget that eerie scene, so would I never forget that afternoon when he told me that tale and a few others besides.

Thankfully, the old fella had written all of this into a book, entitled Bothy to Big Ben. I have a copy beside me now, and with pride I will reproduce what is written inside the front cover, word for word.

"To Andy

who looks as if he's going to get as much fun out of showing cattle as I've had & if he does he'll be like me, a 'lucky laddie'

With all the best for your future

Ben Coutts

Hamburg, Oct 94"

He forgot to add the word *Legendary* before his name….for he was.

Among the other 'guests' at this monumental event were the gregarious team of Ken Fletcher and John Fraser from the Scottish Farmer magazine - whose splendid company kept us laughing continually – I never tire of sharing a dram with Fletch, he always has a story to tell. Besides that duo, there was Ross Muir and Arthur Anderson from BBC Scotland's Landward TV programme, who were making a film of the event and Charlie Wilson from Osmonds Animal Health, to name but a few.

As Bill drove us around on a farm tour in his new Range-rover, it was evident that he and his wife had very much fallen on their feet in this new job. After an hour or two of seeing huge flat fields full of quality stock, Bill pulled out his mobile phone and ordered a round of drinks from the local pub.

You put a round in by phone..?

Indeed. The beer in that part of the world is very frothy, hence you order it 15 minutes in advance. Yes, Bill certainly had it sussed.

The next day I toiled at grooming and presenting the animals, firstly for a show which was judged by the master judge – yep, you got him – Ben Coutts. As well as Highlands, Baumer had new breed called Aubrac, a hard skinned type of creature from France. For a laugh I led one of these into a class to be judged by Ben and his eyes nearly popped out.

'What on *earth* is that thing..?' he muttered under his breath, before placing it last in the class. Later that evening I heard him chastising Baumer for presenting the offensive animal telling him that it would:

'…never be any use as long as it has a hole in its arse.'

It tickled me as I recalled big Fred Harrington's very sentiments from nearly 20 years earlier about the Charolais. Only, in this case, Ben was right.

Later that evening, after a successful sale of stock, Herr B and his lovely wife, Erica, put on one of the most fabulous banquets I have even attended.

Salmon and lobster - flown in especially from Scotland - beef, beef and more beef, the finest quality red wine money could buy, all flowed so plentifully it was almost obscene.

After a short speech from the host, Ben stood up to make a toast.

In his wonderful broadcasting-voice, Ben said a few nice words thanking the host for such a wonderful feast and hospitality. Then, giving the hostess a cheeky smile he finished something like this.

'…*for many years I worked among the Angus cattle breed. In cattle, as in humans, the best cows are bred in tight families. The Angus has three such great families, the Georgina's, the Princess's and the greatest of them all….*' Ben raises his glass, '*…the **Erica's**.*'

Quick as a flash, the hostess pipes up in perfect English.

'Are you saying I look like a COW?!'

On one of the few occasions that Ben has ever been stuck for words, he simply retorted, as he sat down glowing with embarrassment: 'I love you..!'

Before we leave Germany, I had promised to recall a brief story about the late Charles Wilson. The following morning, all a little the worse for wear, Charlie arrives down to the breakfast table a little bleary-eyed and starts looking through the cupboards. After watching in silence for a few minutes, I question him on what else he could possibly need, as breakfast was already laid out.

'The Pledge..' replies Charles, '…has anyone seen the Pledge.'

Baffled as to why this man would require furniture polish at this hour, I raised an eyebrow. Eventually there came the answer.

'I'm looking for the Pledge…because I want to sign it this morning!'

Chapter 200 – Captain Chaos

I know, it's not very nice is it?

But that's what they called me at Ritchey Tagg, mainly behind my back. Can't imagine why…

In hindsight, I probably didn't make a very good employee, I was far too headstrong to be told what to do by anyone other than my mother. And I rarely listened to her.

In my first full season the wheels on the exhibition unit barely touched the ground as we sped around the country visiting every event that would have us. At the time, the company had 5 sales reps who, between them, covered the whole of UK. On a mission to proportionally visit the whole cattle-showing nation, my able and weary secretary, Liz, booked us into just about every county show available. Depending which section of the country it fell into, the local rep would join me. As many of these events were at least 2 or 3 days long, with a day beforehand to set up and another to strip them down, each show blocked out a full week of the calendar. Couple that with a return to the office in North Yorkshire to re-stock and re-order, there wasn't a lot of time to visit home. In that first year, I spent 240 nights away from my own bed – leaving my wife and 2 sons, now 6 and 3 years old, to fend for themselves. For that, I will always feel eternally guilty.

Based loosely on my designs, the company had commissioned a brand new exhibition unit to be built which encompassed a small kitchen and sleeping area. To save money, this was my bed during the summer months, which suited me fine. That meant that I got to sleep on the showground rather than carted off to a soulless hotel – and the showground was where the parties were. The ones that had no closing time. Most mornings I would roll out of bed just in time to open the tarpaulins and greet the customers with bleary eyes – me not them – and a bad head.

If the event was in the south, I would be joined by Dennis, a sober chap, if not a little dull, who would rarely join us in the evenings for a beer if he could help it. In the Midlands it was Andrew, always there with a smile although very particular about appearance and presentation. Wales had its own man, Huw, a likeable young fellow, well-known and popular amongst his own kind, and in Northern England was another Andrew – who is now head of the company. Covering Scotland AND Northern Ireland was Mark, whom I have mentioned previously. Each one would accompany me for the duration, and I would generally delegate them to converse with some of the more boring clients who shuffled in, wanting to know the finer points if an RD2000 sheep tag and *'did they do one in sky-blue-brown colour?'* To be fair to Mark, he did try to brighten them up with a joke or two, often with hilarious consequences.

Our two main directors would occasionally pop up for a day, especially at the Royals, usually because they had just taken exclusivity on some new gadget or other from which they were going to make a fortune. This invariably turned out to be hopelessly impractical – such as a wheel-barrow calving device, of which I think we sold all of 2 – and one of those broke on its first use.

Charlie, I am guessing you don't know what a calving jack is? Well, in the interests of breeding bigger and bigger animals, cows are often mated with bulls of twice their size. During gestation, as the cow eats its way through an entire feed store, the calf inside sometimes grows to impossible proportions.

Hmm, I bet you wish you hadn't asked now?

When calving time eventually arrives, often the issue of getting it out alive would be something that nature would prevent. If left to natural selection, possibly all cows would be easy-calvers but human nature doesn't work that way.

In Bed With Cows

Hence, the requirement of intervention by agriculture's answer to a midwife - a broad-shouldered farmer with biceps like girders and, if the cow is lucky, armed with a device that contains enough ratchets and ropes to pull a Sherman tank out of a quagmire. If she is a little less lucky, a four wheel motor-bike is fastened on the end of it.

Eyes watering yet? Hmmm, mine too.

It gets worse.

Some crazy Swedish scientist, with a brain the size of the London Orbital but with absolutely zero amount of common-sense, had decided that in the interests of a calf being born in this method, it would be quite handy to be able to transport the new offspring somewhere, once it hit the ground.

Of *course*, the answer was to combine a calving-jack with a wheelbarrow into one handy machine.

The whole idea was insanely ludicrous, particularly that this thing, looking like something off the set of a Star Wars movie, cost a few thousand quid when you could buy a wheel-barrow from Midland Shires Farmers for a tenner.

For an intelligent man running a highly successful business, our Managing Director did mange to be pick up some bum products, but I am guessing even he may now see the error of his ways with this one.

Never-the-less, we had to lug the damn thing around the country, taking up space and giving me a near hernia every time I had to load it into the back. I did consider dragging the bloody thing behind the trailer for a while, possibly with a dead calf in it, to demonstrate some additional uses, but thought better of it.

That wasn't the only one either. I am not sure where Geoff met all these loonies, but another guy rocked up with an aerosol can of lacquer which, if sprayed onto the hoof of every cow in the world, would eliminate foot problems forever and save the farmer thousands.

And it only cost 20 quid for a 200ml can. Bargain.

With some sensational marketing, put together by an agency more used to selling ladies fashion, Hoof-wonder (name changed to tect the product) was launched on the agricultural public.

The omission of some practical detail, like the fact that every day Mr Shit-Kicker-Stockman would need undertake and a few hours washing the feet of all his cows when they came in from the clarty meadows, and then spray this highly toxic product on to their feet without getting his nose bashed in, was possibly the biggest oversight since Goliath had underestimated the accuracy of a small Welshman wielding a sock!

Somewhere in Yorkshire, I suspect their may still be warehouse full of these tins left unsold, with a nuclear half-life of another 100 years.

Then there was the gas-fired calf dehorner. This really *was* a brilliant gadget – when it worked. Made in Ireland, sales figures of this natty little unit continually exceeded expectations for the first 6 months - until they started breaking.

Then for the next 4 years, angry farmers would stride on to the stand demanding their money back. After each event, we would end up with crates full of returned de-horners, along with a pallet of broken 'un-breakable' sheep crooks that had snapped the first time they had caught anything bigger than a 3 day old lamb. The party-line for dealing with this problem was that we were to accuse the customer of mal-use and tell him to piss-off and stop whining.

Perhaps not the best way to endear your average farmer when you relied on his custom for a million ear-tags each year?

But despite all this, the company went from strength to strength, mainly on the back of its viral sales of small plastic tags, which had now become compulsory to be fitted in the ear of every 4 legged animal in Europe, thanks to the French. Not only that, but it was repeat business as animals, cattle in particular, with nothing else to do except chew their cud and gaze moronically into space, spent most of their time trying to get them out. So the farmer would have to buy some more…at four times the price of the original ones because they had to be 'specially' printed.

Think of them as the forerunner of Ryanair charging you 10 quid to print your boarding pass.

Probably our most memorable trip was the July 'World Tour' of Scotland. Starting off in Kelso one particular year, we grouped up with a few other trade exhibitors and formed a convoy which kept us continually on the road for 3 weeks. Among the party were the large-as-life Gary Rawlinson, then with Farmers Guardian and who later took over my role at Ritchey. His humour fitted right in with that of Mark and I – his attitude too, where life was about having fun with work fitted around it. The other two in the tour party were Isa Lloyd, an ex world sheep-shearing champion from Wales who marketed his own range of sheep handling equipment, and the late Bob Tyler, a gentleman of gentlemen who had designed an incredible mobile cattle handling set-up which weighed about 500 tons.

On our very first night, with Floors Castle as a backdrop, deep friendships were formed as we huddled into a caravan to witness one of the most spectacular lightening displays I have ever seen.

Suspicious that this was the start of a trademark 3 week summer downpour, I had already wondered at the wisdom of us taking on such an expedition, but thankfully it didn't last. Being a Borders man, this was Mark's local stomping ground and thus, when a few of his mates paid us a visit, next day the party started early.

From there, a 2 hour drag up to Perth before we settled on to a rather boggy showground, our first stop into Vicky Wines for replenishments was already required.

A month or two earlier, over laden with sales stock on my way to the Royal Highland, I had managed to roll the exhibition unit on the A66 just outside Brough. In my defence, I will say that the design of that 4 metre trailer was a disaster waiting to happen, with all the weight stacked far too high above the axles.

At a mere 50 mph, the thing started pushing me down a long bank and then snaking like an angry viper until I could see it out of the side window. Inevitably over it went with a mighty crash, and thankfully didn't turn my 4x4 with it. As the roof peeled open like a tin of cat-food, Ritchey products flew in all directions, spreading our wares across the duel carriageway like confetti in a churchyard. As often happens in such situations, a few local young-farmers heard the crash and came to investigate, retrieving a fair personal haul in the process, before dragging the unit to the side of the road to let a 5 mile backlog of vehicles passed.

I was always disappointed in that event, blaming myself for not keeping it under control, although the design had been technically flawed. Despite applying some modifications, a few years later one of the other lads tipped it over again, and again after that. That comforted me somewhat - the whole thing was obviously a bloody disaster.

Anyway, as a result of my trashing our regular show-unit, we had hired another one, which was much lighter and more stable, and it was this that we took on tour. Whereas the previous unit had a small kitchen area that seated 3 bums at a push and the rest used to carry stock, this one was more of a hospitality unit, with internal comfortable seating of the kind you might find in a cosy pub.

With Mark and myself as landlords!

And, as any landlord will tell you, once you get a full pub, its kinda hard to get folks to leave without being rude. Basically, unknowing to us when we set out, we had hit the road with a travelling bar.

Customers, many of whom were good friends, would come along to the show, visit us by 11am and still be there in our stand at 4 or 5, pissed as Catholics. Then sometimes a guy, who was possibly on his only day off in the whole year, would arrive at the stand pathetically proffering his broken dehorner and sheep crook that his missus had bought him for Christmas, along with a bag of disintegrated ear-tags, to see if he was entitled to a refund. Feeling sorry for the likes, we would shove a tin of John Smiths in his hand, entertain him with a rude joke and direct him to the seating area in a bid to redeem ourselves and our bosses.

Then there was the other type of customer, the know-it-all hobby farmer. You know, him with the goatee beard, bright coloured kagool and lace up walking boots? An expert on all walks of farming, despite only having 3 jacob ewes and an allotment.

It wasn't you, was it Charlie?

I hope not, because inevitably we were quite rude to this person, as he droned on and on about his foot-paring shears that had lost their edge after only three years or the fact that his pig-marker had melted when he had left it in the sun. Well, we weren't exactly rude, not in a nasty way. To us, these folks were just a chance to have a laugh – very much at their expense.

We would play ridiculous games where we would need to include as many song titles in the conversation as possible while keeping a straight face, all the while scoring points. So wrapped up in his own importance, the benign customer would never even notice. One, man, I swear he visited every show we ever went to, with his same broken sheep-shear, used to nod appreciatively whenever he heard the words 'hit me with your rhythm stick' as though he knew exactly what we were talking about!

It was pure class in the most juvenile of ways.

On other occasions, we would completely fabricate new words, the longer the better.

After inspecting the broken gadget for a few seconds, one of us would take a deep breath and then continue something like this:

'Well, Mr Edwards, it is intrivically umbrilacious that you should craffer us with such a simbule contrabatation – I imprond to convibulate it with my contribes. We will fanticulate you shortly – good day!'

All the while the man is nodding, thankful that he getting such excellent service from these well educated chaps.

Meanwhile, up in the exhibition unit, a few pals, such as Garry, would be stifling guffaws as they awarded marks for our efforts like a scorer in an Olympic gymnast discipline!

We would also have the knack of finishing each others sentences which is outrageously annoying to anyone who is trying to extract a sensible answer to a simple question.

When we weren't annoying the general public, we were watching them instead. People-watching is, I am sure, the hobby of many, but we would take it to another level. Anyone slightly out of the norm, whatever the norm is, would be a target for our infantile but highly entertaining observations and we would crack ourselves up whenever a badly dressed person passed by – or anyone with a silly walk. It certainly passed the time.

We also used to attribute nicknames to people, which were very often more befitting than their real name. On one occasion, in Oban actually, we had a late night out with a chap til the small hours until suddenly, he disappeared. Now, as you know, Oban is on the sea and for a while we attempted to track him down before we gave up and heartlessly carried on without him. The next day, this fellow was due to meet us somewhere and he never showed. Convinced he had obviously fallen to his peril in the Firth, we guessed he must be somewhere bobbing up and down out in the harbour. So I named him Bob. Eventually, he did turn up, a day later with some feeble excuse saying he had been called away on business, when we were pretty sure he must have been so drunk the night before that he was confined to his bed for the day. To this day, I am not sure of his real name and even when I saw him a few months ago, I still call him Bob.

After each one of these events a massive dance would be held – usually in a marquee somewhere on or near the showground. Invariably, we would be in attendance, although often they were so crowded that there was little room to even raise a glass, let alone your knees in an interesting dance manoeuvre.

On one occasion, as we all drank from beer cans, there was a kafuffle near-by where we were standing and a young man dropped to the ground. It transpired that he had swallowed a wasp with his beer which had then stung him in the throat. Sadly we were informed the next day that the poor chap had died on his way to hospital. It did put the dampers on proceedings for a day or two - and since that day I have never drunk directly from a tin of beer on a hot day ….

In a bid to give our liver a short rest, one evening we decided to go to the local water-park for a swim and a sauna. With a well appointed gym and its convoluted array of water-slides, we zoomed around the place having races to see who could get down the slides the fastest. Now Isa Lloyd was a somewhat portly fellow and, not to put too fine a point on it, a little un-aerodynamic. After timing the rest of us down the steepest slide at around ten seconds, on Isa'a turn the time extended into a couple of minutes – and still he didn't appear. Duly a search party was despatched, only to find that the poor chap had got stuck inside the chute like Winnie the Pooh in the honey tree! Except, as he lay there feet first, the water was cascading over his head nearly downing him. Thankfully with an extra push he was freed and torpedoed down the remainder of the route in record time.

From Perth we made our way up to Turriff show when, for some inexplicable reason I decided to buy a bike. From then on, I would cycle my way around each event, reporting back on anything that was worth a second look. I also used it to go to the pub that evening which was probably something of a mistake as I fell off it so many times on the way home that it had little paint left and me missing chunks of skin.

Years later I would ride it through the streets of Amsterdam – where I lived for a short while – and do the same. I still have it, in fact.

From Turriff it was a short hop to Nairn and from there to the Black Isle where I had kicked off my stint of employment a few years earlier. Conveniently all these shows were as in perfect chronological sequence as they were in geographical succession across the North East.

Leaving Mark behind, I then pulled into Invergordon, just north of Aberdeen and anchored up, ready to catch a boat – to Orkney.

Nestled in the Cromarty Firth there were, at the time, dozens of disused oilrigs anchored just off shore. On each one of these rigs lived a skeleton crew of 3 men, a sparky, a chippy and a technician of some kind. What a life that must have been, isolated like that for weeks on end? There are only so many games of cards a man can play.

In Bed With Cows

And what if you didn't like the other two?

In a situation like that, there was only really one thing they could do – and that was to drink.

After a tiring week I rolled the unit to a halt near the waters edge and climbed in the back to get a few hours sleep before the cargo ferry was due to leave. On the other side of this makeshift car-park was a local bar and from inside came the usual chatter of late night drinkers.

Just as I was dozing off, outside I heard some noise and pulled the curtain back to see three men propping each other up, staggering across the tarmac. A more unsteady trio I can scarcely imagine – it was like a script from the Three Stooges. Once again, I wished I had a video camera but back then mobile phones were as big as house-bricks and the only apps they contained were to ring people up.

Come to think of it, these three men at that precise moment probably had the combined mental capacity of a house-brick, as they attempted a ladder down to the water and a waiting dinghy, 20 feet below.

For this was their journey home, back to their rig to endure yet another day playing cards or hide-n-seek.

Very soon, the inevitable happened.

SPLASH!

Some shouting followed.

'..you 'right there, Jock?'

Silence. Then…

SPLASH - off went the second one.

By this time, I had gathered my wits and run to help.

Should I call the coast-guard? Or the pub landlord?

Just as I reached the edge, I heard a tiny engine start up and could just make out a body climbing up into the dinghy.

Within minutes, all three of them were safely aboard and the little rubber craft put-putted its way out to sea.

Later, when chatting to a local whilst we were boarding the ancient cargo vessel, I relayed the incident to him.

'Oh, aye...that's quite normal....'

Seemingly they lose two or three personnel per year during the nightly trip back from the bar, but nobody was too alarmed.

'...they hae to go to the pub, else they'd go mad, ya kin...'

Go Mad?

What could be madder that getting absolutely stocious, climbing down a 20 foot slippery ladder into a tiny unstable rubber boat in total darkness, and then falling in the North sea after midnight? Every night!

I don't think Health and Safety had reached this far North at that time.

At around 1.30am, after reversing the 20 foot unit through 500 yards of darkness into a space between containers with only a few inches either side, I was once again in my life sharing a tiny bedroom with a total stranger. However, unlike the one at the Royal Show from the beginning of this book, this was a large and greasy Aberdonian trucker who could have snored and farted for Scotland. With that and the boat rocking like a whore's headboard, I got absolutely no sleep whatsoever and it seemed like two eternities had passed by the time we rolled into Kirkwall at 10am.

Still sleeping wasn't an option because as soon as we disembarked, I pulled the show unit into a parking space and jumped on to a waiting speedboat, heading off for lunch.

I felt like James Bond as we headed off through the

In Bed With Cows

surf at 50 knots, my curly locks trailing behind me, towards a massive stone castle perched on the cliffs of the neighbouring island of Shapensay. The skipper and owner of this impressive piece of machinery was my good pal Chris – or Dr Z – as we affectionately knew him. As we approached the magnificent building, with its pointed turrets and roof battlements, I at least expected Dr Z to let out an evil laugh and guide us into an underground cave. But he didn't, instead delivering me to the front door of the castle to be welcomed by his enchanting and extremely elegant mother.

Chris and I had been pals for quite some time and we would often share trade stands together at some of the smaller shows. His family was steeped in history, since his father, originally from Polish aristocracy, had escaped from a Prisoner of War camp whilst being marched towards Auschwitz and had then set up a resistance army based on the Orkney Isles. Leaving his brother to run their large farm, Balfour Mains, after a few careers including lobster fishing off Cape Wrath, Chris has set up a company dealing in Veterinary Instruments. We had also recently taken a trip to Paris, but the story of that adventure can hang on for another time.

Meeting up with my boss once more, who had flown in for the occasion, and dining on local fish with a few other members of his family, the shutters were starting to fall over my eyes. After an intense evening, fuelled by excessive quantities of Highland Park whisky, I eventually made my weary way up the monumental staircase past suits of armour on every turn to a bedroom big enough to stage a football tournament.

It was one of those pinch-yourself moments as I marvelled at the splendour of it all while the room rotated around me.

Next day, Chris drove me around that wonderful fertile island, stopping in at a neighbouring farm, Quoymorehouse, to take morning coffee with one Tommy Lesley, and admire the fabulous quality of his commercial cattle herd. When I questioned him why the quality of cattle was so much higher on these Islands than anywhere else in the UK, he supplied me a simple philosophy that many a cattleman should heed.

'All our beasts have to make that trip across the water to the mainland. The cost of transport is the same for a bad one as a good one – so we might as well keep good ones…'

Makes perfect sense to me.

Back to Kirkwall by late afternoon in time to set up the exhibition unit for Orkney County show – one of the best one days shows in UK. What it loses in size, it sure makes up with quality, in all its stock and its folk. Once again we offered hospitality to a host of well-known farmers from across the North of Scotland where, sitting in my unit, business deals were done and whisky taken plentifully.

That day I made a good few friends on the island and one day I will keep my promise and go back there to visit them. Get the kettle on, Liam!

Chapter 201 – Responsibility

Now there's a word I never thought I would use – not when applying it to myself, anyway.

Having not long started my fledgling career as a stockman, by the time I was 17 I had already applied and been accepted to join the committee of our local show – in Tenbury Wells, Worcestershire.

I will admit that Tenbury is no sprawling metropolis but each and every event of this type, no matter how small, relies on a group of well-meaning and hard working volunteers to keep it going and I was quite prepared to offer my services.

Then, with a couple of years basic organising experience under my belt, I took a larger step upwards – to the committee of the Birmingham (still in Stafford) primestock show. Aged merely 19, it was my intention to right some of the few problems that I saw with this event which, to my mind, was run by a bunch of old farts. The fact that I was the youngest council member by about 40 years did nothing to quell my enthusiasm.

At my very first meeting, when introduced as this young whippersnapper who thought he knew best, I announced to them that I was there to stick up for the stockman who often got a rough deal. It didn't go down too well and were it not for a few friendly faces such as Jack Bedell and John Weyman-Jones, I'm sure I might have been evicted immediately.

When minutes were read out from sub-committees of finance and accounts, the speaker would need to raise his voice to be heard above the noise of snoring coming from top-table after a decadent lunch of smoked salmon and jolly fine port. As you can imagine, with a naïve eagerness to make things better, this rankled with me somewhat.

Patiently, I awaited my turn until the subject of Livestock Stewards arose, on which I pounced.

'Mr Speaker,' said I, boldly, knees-a-tremble, 'compared to other events I have attended, and they are plentiful, I would like to tell you that, from my experience, the cattle stewarding at Birmingham (in Stafford) Primestock show is pretty shit.'

As you can guess, this extracted gasps even from the sleeping octogenarians in the front row, and especially from one man who *was*, as I was well aware, one *of* the stewards.

'Explain yourself or begone,' was pretty much their response, but one for which I was ready and armed. As I read out a list of their failings, some of which pointed fingers pretty accurately, the room fell to silence. By the time I was through with my little speech, red-faced and passionate, there was a mumbling rippling round the room like a clanging gong in a cathedral.

Eventually the question: 'What do you propose we do to address this, you cheeky young scallywag?' was proffered.

Before I could stop myself, the words came out all too quickly. 'If the board will back me up, I would like to offer my services as a cattle steward at the next event.'

After some more mutterings, a show of hands was taken and, reluctantly by some, I was voted in by just one vote.

For all I was quite pleased to get some recognition for my organisation skills, I was also aware that it would be a difficult job because I was actually an exhibitor at the event as well. From now on I would be a player/manager and juggling the two jobs would demand some precision.

At that time it was traditional that all the ring-stewards

wore bowler hats – I believe they still do - and that was something I was definitely NOT going adhere to. With my eighties style long hair hanging in ringlets, this was obviously not going to be a good look – unless they wanted Mark Bolan at their service.

However, I had no qualms with the ring-stewards who were a reasonably switched on bunch and had no intention of muscling in on that side of proceedings. No, to me the inherent problem lay with the dozy ones whose job it was to help exhibitors by affording them enough warning to get to the right animal to a collecting ring on time. Thus avoid the chaos that was currently going on.

Charlie, if I can elaborate on this a little. A large cattle show such as this one would have two main rings, both being judged at the same time by two different judges. Generally, as these judges would work at variable speeds, it was near impossible to estimate at what time each animal would be required for their turn on the sawdust. And cattle grooming – which I am sure my cohorts will back me up on – is all about timing. In the same way that Miss World – yes her again – needs her make-up set at the precise moment before she parades into the spotlights, so do our fashionable cows.

Genuinely I believe, at my very first appointment, I made a considerable difference at Stafford that year, because I was aware of who was who and, more importantly, who was where. It wasn't difficult; it purely took a little understanding of the needs of the exhibitor and a strong short-term memory.

Up until that occasion, most of the bleary eyed old buffers that were in that role would have no better idea of what any of the exhibitors looked like, let alone where their animals were stalled, than they would know all the words of Don Maclean's American Pie. Having said that, I am not sure anyone knows **all** the verses – it does go on a bit!

Let me just point out here that I am not *really* a committee man, despite this and a few other appointments.

Unlike the majority of council members who are mostly out for a free lunch and a chat among their comrades, the sole purpose for me was to make a difference and try to mend what was broken.

I would like to think that I did that – for a good few years anyway – in Stafford.

The next step was to be *'one giant leap for me-kind!'*

As you may recognise, I always speak as I find, especially about people I have known reasonably well.

To me, the late Jack Bedell was a great man.

Kind and gentle, as understanding and fair as he was innovative and entrepreneurial. You may recall in the opening pages of this book, he was the one who first brought Limousin cattle to UK. Not a bad accolade to have on your epitaph and one for which he received an OBE for.

As well as sitting on the committee for Birmingham show, Jack was also the representative for our area – the Midlands and Wales – for Royal Smithfield.

As his three year stint in this role was coming to a close I asked him if he wouldn't mind backing a campaign to get me elected in his absence - and that he did, with grace.

Selection for such an honoured position came down to a democratic vote from those members who resided in the area – and there were quite a few of them. Ballot papers were duly sent out and - although thankfully I never resorted to wearing one of the gawky ghastly rosettes that politicians lower themselves to – I made a few calls to help canvass a few votes. Not house-calls, you understand – and definitely no kissing babies in front of the camera - but pleading for support nonetheless.

Evidently, I didn't plead hard enough.

After waiting on tenterhooks for a few weeks,

eventually I got a letter to say that I had not received enough votes on this occasion, being out-polled by – also the late - David Mathews from South Wales.

However, after a recent meeting of one of their sub-committees, it had been decided that I was the kind of calibre they were looking for amongst their ranks and thus, they had used their power to co-opt me onto their council – for one year – after which I would then stand for re-election to a 3 year term.

Whoopie-bollocking-doo and slap me with a wet fish..!

Me, sitting on the board of what I deemed to be one of the greatest institutions on earth. For 200 years, this organisation had been running thanks to having such great minds amongst its organisers.

It took a while to sink in.

Unlike Birmingham show, Smithfield was run by men of stature and recognition, many of whom were peers of the realm. That doesn't necessarily make them any better at their job, I grant you, a fact which could be possibly attributed to the show's eventual demise from its traditional London location – although that is perhaps a tad unfair.

For my first meeting I arrived, suited and booted, at the Farmers club in Whitehall and was totally overawed by the occasion. Down its long corridors of power, walls were adorned with oil-paintings of great farmers from a by-gone era. Jethro Tull, Turnip Townsend and Robert Bakewell, they were all there in their own hall of fame.

Actually, I'm not sure if Turnip Townsend was there, I just put that in because I liked the name. I can remember it from school, when old Turnip was the spark that started the agricultural revolution by rotating his crops from field to field.

Turnip crops, obviously.

A simple concept really – I'm quite surprised someone hadn't thought of it earlier.

Having just looked him up, I am actually jolly glad he wasn't there in person. Here is a quote from the turnip website:

"Although Townshend's contemporaries describe him a bore because of his overzealous chatter about agriculture, it cannot be denied that his agricultural reforms were greatly helpful." Yawn – is that the time?

Anyway, I digress.

As I entered the Sir William Cumber room, Sir William Cumber senior looked down from the giant canvass on the wall while his grandson William Cumber jnr – then the show's chairman - welcomed me to the room.

It was a rather bizarre moment, to say the least.

However, regardless of all the pomp and ceremony I was expecting, these were a friendly bunch of chaps who made me most welcome. Obviously, having been an exhibitor at the event for many years, I knew a good percentage of them as they had herded me around in the past. It was a bit daunting though – the realisation that I was probably the only one in the room whose name didn't appear in Burkes Peerage coupled with the fact that I was not even worthy of enough votes to elevate myself to such a position.

I need not have worried.

That was the first time I had met William Cumber, a highly intelligent chap always ready with a smile that helped me feel at ease, and whose immense farming operation spans most of the Home Counties. Alongside him was Sir Richard Cooper, head of the Coopers Animal Health dynasty, with whom I later became great friends. Sadly Richard was killed in a car accident some years after.

Among them were also faces more familiar to me such as John Campbell – a well respected sheep breeder from Northumberland - and Donald MacPherson, already a regular winner in the show-ring, both of whom I considered – and still do – as good friends.

On that occasion, our Patron, none other than the Queen Mother herself, was not present although she was a regular visitor to the show itself.

The year previous I had been exhibiting an Angus steer of my own which had won a first prize – one of only three I ever achieved with my own stock at Smithfield. As well as patron of Smithfield, the QM was also President of the Aberdeen Angus Cattle society – having a strong herd of her own at Castle of Mey.

When she did her rounds – hmm, that makes her sound like a paper-boy!? – of the stock-lines she always made a b-line for the Angus and so it was that I stood by my beast waiting patiently for her to arrive.

In the distance, I could see my mother and father witnessing the occasion, the old man carrying his omnipresent video camera. After gaining quick permission from the chief steward, I signalled to Mum to come and stand by me.

When my turn came to be introduced to Her Majesty, which I had been on numerous occasions before, I took the liberty of introducing My Mum to The Queen Mum.

Not many people can say they have done that.

A photograph capturing this moment holds pride of place on my wall and always makes me proud when I glance at it.

'Do you have many Angus cattle?' asks HRH of Ma.

'Just a small herd, Maam,' she shakily replies.

We Fraziers are nothing if not masters – or mistresses on this occasion – of over-estimation.

For a small herd, read ONE. And it was standing right behind us!

For some reason, with a twinkle in those wonderful sky-blue eyes of hers, I felt that the QM knew that.

Anyway, once again I digress.

I won't bore you with all the details of my stint on Smithfield council, which spanned ten years, save to say that it introduced me to some wonderful people, numerous Royalty among them, who I am honoured to say I have worked with.

A few chapters earlier I casually threw in the comment that I retired from cattle-grooming in the mid nineties, partly because I had achieved most of my goals at the sport.

The real reason was that – two years later – I was promoted to the role of Smithfield show cattle steward.

They even gave me a badge with my name on it!

Had they known some of the antics that yours truly had been up to downstairs or – heaven forbid – read this book, I am not so sure the appointment would have been so forthcoming, but there I was, in the brochure.

Before I colour in a little more of what this role entailed, let me just add one last story from those glorious days in the dungeon before I let it go completely.

You will need to picture the scene with me to make this work.

Here we go….

In the maze that is the basement of that vast building, one main corridor passes the door of dormitory A and extends for some 500 metres until it meets another one, which connects the hall with a nearby underground railway station.

You may even have walked along it.

Each morning, many people – commuters and show visitors alike - do.

Now sometimes, due to the stress and heat of an indoor event such as Smithfield, animals occasionally get taken ill. In a bid to revive them with some slightly fresher air, a small wooden pen was erected each year, out near the main entrance. Although rarely used, this ***isolation*** box, as it is known, is about 3 metres square with low sides so the poorly creature can be kept an eye on.

Despite, in my opinion, London holding absolutely no fresh-air whatsoever, the position of the isolation box is right next to the main thoroughfare mentioned above.

You with me so far?

Got a rough idea of the geography?

OK.

A very, very late night 'up-town' found me stumbling to my bed at around 6am. Don't ask me where I had been, I honestly couldn't tell you if you did. Being 50 feet underground and nestled amongst a mass of great heating pipes that supplied the exhibition hall above, dormitory A was always stifling hot. Hence, no pyjamas required inside a reasonably well insulated sleeping bag.

'Snore, snore!' went this soon-to-be-appointed council member.

Vaguely I sensed an awareness of movement, but not enough to wake me from my slumbers, as not one but six of my compatriots raised my whole bed to their shoulders.

Like an unorthodox funeral procession, these six burly chaps carried the bed out through the door in a silent slow march, down said 500 metre corridor, out onto the main drag and deposited it – **in the fucking isolation box**!

With one Andy Frazier still asleep in it at 9am!

Eventually I opened my eyes to see streams of pedestrians walking past and having a quick peek inside.

Bastards!!

I have to admit, I did see the funny side of it and I even waved to a few of the Londoners as though it was a quite normal practice.

But, I now had another major problem.

If you recall the snippet of info I confided to you earlier, inside the sleeping-bag I was start-bollock naked – and a long way from home.

Charlie, have you ever tried to shuffle 700 metres in a sleeping bag?

I have.

And, believe me, its not easy!

As luck would have it, a large chocolate coloured fellow came wondering past pushing a sack-trolley.

My saviour.

With a grin the width of Marble Arch and me perched precariously on a beer crate, he delivered me back to the dorm to be greeted by fits of laughter!

No-one owned up to being a pole-bearer at the event, but my suspicions for at least one of them lay with a certain Pete Bodily. Fair justice repaid, Pete..

As it happens, through no fault of our jokes and activities, that was the last year we slept in the dungeons of Earls Court, as the following year Health and Safety condemned it out of all existence and we were forced to take umbrage in a few local hotels in the area.

Having spent many an evening in its crammed bar, from then on, my hotel of choice was the Mowbray Court, a few hundred metres from the main door to the event.

This small but acceptable hotel on Penywern road was and still is run by two brothers of Scandinavian origin who were extremely tolerant of our late night drinking and the noise that accompanied it, which would often continue after 5am. I suppose the fact that they were taking thousands of pounds per night over the bar contributed to this fact but, nonetheless, it cannot have been easy dealing with a scrum of hundreds of mainly Scottish farmers full to the brim with whisky for six continual nights.

One chap, who has requested to remain nameless, although he has already featured earlier in this book, holds the accolade of being awoken by the sound of the hoover, just in time for breakfast while sleeping overnight on a bench in the bar – FOURR mornings running!

Good effort – D-Mac!

Sometimes, when I visit Earls Court Exhibition for other events, it seems strange dropping into the Mowbray for a pint and seeing it totally empty and calm.

Although us stock exhibitors tended to block-book the entire hotel, sometimes there would be the odd booking from a 'civilian' who was blissfully unaware that the farmers were in town in that December week.

Can you imagine how this must have seemed to them?

A few of them took it on the chin and attempted to join in the revelry but more often others took offence to the rather un-political language that would spill out towards the street.

Although I am in no way racist, occasionally some of the other farmers might have been. Farming in UK isn't a particularly multi-cultural business.

'Oi, Sinbad…' called out a rather drunken Hereford cattle breeder one evening to a well dressed Asian man sitting at the end of the bar, dripping in gold chains, who evidently wasn't of agricultural background.

'where the f'ing 'ell do you come from….?'

'Saudi Arabia…' replied the man, humbly.

'..well, with all that f'ing oil, it must be your f'ing round!'

As you can imagine, I just wanted the whole bar to open up and swallow me immediately. But to be fair to the guy, although grossly insulted, he did put his hand in his pocket and bought Fred a drink and they shook hands.

1998 was my first year of stewarding at Smithfield which by then had become a bi-annual event.

The job started on Thursday evening and finished a week later and during that entire time, I considered that I was on duty, day and night. It was an extremely tiring but highly rewarding experience. Not financially rewarding, you understand, purely voluntary but with basic expenses taken care of.

To start with it felt a bit uncomfortable, now being on the other side of the tracks, but I soon settled into it under the steady guidance of our chief, Neil Gourlay. Although some others in our crew tended to hand out orders to exhibitors in a slightly heavy-handed way, mine was always to ask them casually, on the understanding that for much of the time they would be under nervous stress – just like I had been many times in the past. As I may have advocated, Smithfield exhibitors are a seasoned and professional bunch and rarely required any assistance unless rules or locations had changed from what they were accustomed to. But there was always the new-comer who warranted a little extra help in this daunting environment and I, for one, knew exactly how they felt. Likewise, especially on arrival, there would be an animal that was a bit nervous and once again, I felt I had enough experience to offer a physical hand rather than stand back proffering advice.

In the show-ring, things were a little different, and you really had to be on your toes, but again there was a host of experience to help me through. Past masters, Ian Grant and Jim Stobo would step in to oversee proceedings and were always quick to sort a situation, should it arise. Also the level-headed Donald Biggar would never be far away when snap decisions needed making in a diplomatic fashion.

My first championship day did cause me a slight embarrassment though.

It was the very last of those wonderful occasions when HRH, the Queen Mother came and sat in on proceedings. After holding up the judging and her taking centre seat with the best view, operations were commenced, this time with me working under Royal scrutiny.

Unlike any other show I have been involved with, Royal Smithfield was organised with military precision. Each morning lists would be printed out detailing each animal that was required in which order, as well as full instructions for the stewards as to who was doing what at any time. Out of six of us, two stewards were allocated to work inside the main ring while the others made sure that cattle were delivered punctually. One of those two kept an eye on the cattle, my favoured job because I could feel for each and every handler from past experience. When an animal played up or, more often, went on strike I would be by its side in seconds, helping move it along but with minimum fuss. The other job was to look after the judge, making sure you were on hand to answer any questions and lining animals up as and when he required them. This role also entailed collecting the rosettes from the secretary for each class and then giving them to the judge or an appointed dignitary to hand them out.

With the appearance of Britain's oldest and most adored Royal I was given one extra instruction. In order not to obstruct her view, whenever I crossed from one side of the ring to the other, I was not to pass in front of HRH. At the side of the ring, the row of chairs on which she and a few other important people sat had been brought forward from the wall in order that we could pass behind them.

For the svelte Julian, Mike Pullen, Neil and others, this was no problem but, then in my late thirties, I will admit that since giving up handling cattle for a living in favour of a desk job, I had put on a few pounds. Thus the gap was none to wide.

On that occasion, as on most of her public appearances, Elizabeth had selected a very nice blue brimmed hat and it was this that caused me the problem.

Charlie, have you ever knocked the Queen Mother's hat off?

No?

Thankfully, nor have I, but I have come very, very close to it, on a dozen occasions.

Somewhere in the wings, my father was watching, again with his video camera. I have since seen the tape and it is as nerve-wracking as the championship judging itself. In the background all you can here are gasps and my mother's voice saying:

'Oh my God, he's going to knock it off….oh..ohh….phew…!' every time I passed behind the QM. I have investigated what the penalty is for defacing a Royal's attire, but can only assume it would result in yet another stint in the Tower of London followed by a bloody public execution.

Fortunately, I didn't need to.

After judging was over and the silverware handed out, I was privileged to accompany Her Majesty, along with a select party, to a little room known simply as G9, for a little pre-lunch drink. It was an honour I shall never forget. However, there was a little hiccup in proceedings though, as her preferred tipple of choice was not readily available at the bar. *I will not divulge what it was as some things are best kept secret.* Taking swift action, whilst the others kept her talking, I managed to get our barman, under threat of the British Treason Act, to rapidly locate a bottle elsewhere and (Maam's) order was resumed before she realised the problem.

At a subsequent event, once again I fell short with the Royal Family, this time yet another tete-a-tete with the Princess Royal.

On this occasion, the last London event as it happens, I had been promoted to the dizzy heights of Deputy-chief cattle steward. In stock terms, this is almost royalty itself.

With my gleaming badge in place, as Princess Anne arrived at the show ring, she was just in time to see the judging of the Highland cattle. I am not sure if she recognised that it was I whom she had encountered a few years earlier hacking off the hair from one of these beasts like some maniac barber. If she did, she didn't mention it, and I certainly wasn't going to remind her, that was for sure. Instead we had a chat about this and that, me mentioning that my youngest son was in the same school boarding-house as hers had been. Eventually returning to the subject of the four Highland cattle presented in front of her, she requested:

'Are they all from Scotland?'

'Oh, yes, Maam,' I replied, confidently, without double

checking my facts.

Ooops.

While I crossed my fingers behind my back, Anne turned to the handler of the first animal that lined up before her.

'Where abouts are you from, young man?' she enquired.

Please say Glasgow, please say Glasgow…

'Norfolk!' said the chap, in the broadest east England accent imaginable.

Doh!

Turning to me with a killer-frown, she said:

'Well, that's in Scotland, is it?'

At least she was interested in the show though, and its association with the modern livestock industry.

Unlike her brother, Charles.

The very next day, he also made a visit.

Throughout this book, I have often referred to the older, more traditional breeds which for a while during the seventies were on the edge of extinction. In many cases it is only due to the work of the Rare Breeds Survival Trust, started and spearheaded by Joe Henson, father of TV's Adam Henson, that some of them did survive at all.

Many of the better beef breeds that returned to favour, did so by demand for their use amongst the industry, be it for a renewed requirement for hardier hill cows or top end quality beef. However, sitting among a few of those 'rarer' breeds were what was originally defined as a duel-purpose breed – one that could provide dairy milk and beef. A sort of foot in both camps, although not really excelling in either.

A bit like a Liberal government!

The Red Poll is one such breed. With its motley colour and fine bone, it may be a reasonable looking animal but when it comes to meat quality – or quantity – it is never going to shine. I am not expert in the dairy world, but my guess is it won't ever make it to the top producers list in that arena either. Breeds such as these have long been surpassed – or evolved into something more useful.

So it was, that year, that four of this breed turned up at Smithfield. Now bear in mind they probably only had a gene pool of a few dozen to choose from, this was in itself quite a reasonable achievement. Unfortunately, possibly as direct result of them having a tiny gene pool, they were a dreadful example, not just of their breed, but of the bovine species in general.

I don't want to take away credit from Dianne, the lady who provided them - who may well be reading this and then firing up her email browser with sharpened fingernails – for her commendable efforts in reviving a breed from the '*gallows of nature's selection*'. But, in the scheme of things, on that day they kind of stood out awkwardly amongst an otherwise great display of some of the finest beef in the world.

However, it was these and only these that HRH the Prince of Wales was interested in. And that I found a tad disappointing. As I introduced him to a few worthy exhibitors and extolled to him the monumental operation that we had to undertake just to get such a fine display of the future of agriculture into the centre of the capital, he was only interested in looking at what time had forgotten.

In the same way that the Countryfile programme on BBC panders to the *minority* interests of the countryside instead of taking a look at functional, productive and relevant food subjects such as crop prices, beef disease and quality lamb production, so it seems that our next-in-line monarch has his eyes purely focussed on preservation rather than production.

To me, that is quite a worrying thought for our future.

Ooops - Off to the Tower again!

In fact, this book may not even make it past the censors....

Please don't get me wrong, Charlie, I am very much a Royalist, but this is a book full of my own personal experiences.

Maybe I should keep my opinions to myself?

Hmmm? Yeah, right.

Next time will be the first time!

Talking of opinions, later that day I had the pleasure of escorting Clarissa Dixon-Wright around the stock lines. Now there is a lady who is happy to listen and learn, but who sure does call a spade a spade. Also in attendance was Lady Harriet Harman, who had recently been one of the advocates of the Hunting Ban. To show what she thought of that imposition, Clarrie had turned up in a silk blouse emblazoned with a hunting scene across it!

Yep. Pure class, so she is.

As I mentioned, Royal Smithfield, had become a bi-annual event since 1986 as the agricultural industry sunk into yet another recession. This decision had been taken by the Agricultural Traders Association, who ran the majority of that event. Basically, due to its location in central London, the show was becoming massively expensive for exhibitors and trade stand space harder and harder to sell. For a few years, the event had been running at a loss and cutting it to every two years was a way of prolonging the inevitable.

This it did for a further four events but by 2004 rumours were already circulating that this would be the last show in London. Despite my being on the council, I had never been privy to the longer term plans for the event and as far as I was concerned we were signed up for at least one more in 2006.

After the championships that year, a massive party was held, as per every event, in the area allocated for storing the show-boxes. Kists to those north of the border. This was, as it happens a kist party to end all kist parties.

Yeah, yeah, we've all been to parties to end all parties.

Well, this one definitely was, for more reasons than one. Due to the usual Health and Safety nonsense, Earls Court exhibition hall has a strict policy that only exhibitors are allowed in the hall after the show closes at 6pm. Furthermore a rule, possibly invented specifically for this event, was introduced that alcohol was not to be drunk during these hours. With upwards of 300 people, singing, drinking and generally having a good time, this party was a fairly blatant disregard for all of the above rules, as well as perhaps the no smoking rule, London's noise levels and a number of other civil offenses.

But this was Smithfield – the flagship of Earls Court's exhibitions.

Wasn't it?

As per usual, yours truly joined in the revelry and even stood up to make a speech. Hugh Dunlop, who had won that year's event – as well as the previous one – made a speech about his win and personally thanked the stewards for their efforts and commitment. In the absence of our chief, my reply was along the lines of:

'..it's a great pleasure to work with such professionals, and by the way, we'll see you in two years time, despite the rumours…'

This, as you can imagine, brought a rowdy cheer.

In fact, the cheer was loud enough to solicit interest from the security office.

Andy Frazier

Having already been pre-warned about breaking the rules the previous evening, within a few minutes, about 50 rather heavily built security guards arrived to break up the proceedings.

I'm not sure where they had unearthed some of the Neanderthals that immerged and then surrounded the place, but they were definitely 'up for it'! However, after an emotional day and mind-boggling quantities of alcohol, the mostly Scottish stockmen inside, united with their English companions and joined forces, ready to illicit revenge for Culloden, Glencoe, Agencourt, Paschendale and just about any other brutal battle that anyone could recall from the previous millennia.

Beside me, the highly diplomatic Donald Biggar, our vice-chairman that year, raised an eyebrow and then delegated to me a task that was probably the biggest sales job I have ever done. You're the new deputy chief, said he, go and get it sorted.

Thanks, Donald, I still owe you one!

'Who's in charge here', bellowed an aggressive fellow outside, already looking for first blood.

'Fuck off, Sassenachs,' came a united but rather unwise response from inside.

'I am!' said little old me, pushing in front of them and standing all of five foot nine in my heels. 'Is there a problem?'

'You have to get this lot out of here, right now. Or we will come in and remove them ourselves!'

'Come an 'ave a go if you think you're 'ard enough…' comes a helpful chorus from behind me.

'Aw, come on Man, they're just having a bit of fun.' Smiles greasily.

'It's against the rules..'

'Oh, is it? Well so is full-scale warfare, but if you don't remove your bunch of thugs…I mean manly-looking gentlemen here,' more smiles, 'I think there might possibly be a fight?' Reads man's name-badge. 'Do you really want a mass fight on your watch, Luther?'

He considers this

'Because I don't think your Boss would do…'

'You know my Boss?'

'Sure. It was me who appointed your company for this job…' Bluffing turns to bullshit. 'But I am not so sure we would again if you guys instigate a fight…'

What passes for a thought goes through Luther's brain. Before he can quantify this in his own oversized head, I get the upper hand.

'Why don't you take your chaps away, and I will have a word with my guys, eh?' Another greasy smile. 'If I can persuade them to leave, quietly, say within half an hour? Then it will save you calling the entire London ambulance force. Huh?

'Are you threatening me…' Luther has manned up again.

'No Man, come on, you know it makes sense…' Holds out hand to shake.

Luther accepts it and retreats. Disappointedly his gang of thugs follow him in single file to a safe distance, huddling a few hundred metres away.

Back inside the party, I am offered a pat on the back and a dram. Thankfully, some of the more responsible ones among us realise this is the end of the night and start to work on the revellers.

'Lads, if you want this show back here in London, then

we had better disperse..!'

A few at a time, they did, some taunting the waiting gang of blood-thirsty guards as they went but, thanks to me, it all ended peacefully.

But how little did we know…that was a promise too far.

Just over a year later, despite all our reassurances, I got a phone call to say that the Royal Smithfield Show, as we know it, would close…..forever.

It was a call that nearly broke my heart.

That same year, I knew my cattle days would be over, certainly for a good while and, looking for a new start in life, I took a decision to move overseas.

I have no idea how, when or where, but I am pretty certain that one day we will be reunited, those cows and I.

I live in hope.

Epilogue

Just over a year earlier, I had my very last conversation with that great man, Captain Ben – bizarrely in the company of Harry Enfield – before he passed away.

Having then read all of Ben's books, I told him a little secret, of my yearning to be a writer myself one day.

'Don't wait until you're an old codger like me,' he encouraged in his regal fashion, 'get to it straight away. I think you might make a great author – as long as you always write from the heart.'

I would like to thank him for that – and to thank you for reading this.

Believe me, this, my 22nd book did come from my very core.

Finally, I know your name is not really Charlie but, whoever you are, I hope my stereotyped references didn't irritate you too much.

I would like to personally thank you for making it to the end of this book, and trust that it may have slightly changed your outlook on the bovine species.

Please drop me a line, anytime, to: cows@andyfrazier.co.uk so that we can catch up and have a yarn.

Whether you enjoyed this book or not, I would be so so grateful if you would leave a review of it on Amazon. It doesn't take many seconds, but to us authors, reviews are very important as they offer our readers an unbiased opinion. I don't care what you write – if you hated it and it offended you, then it may do the same for others and they need to know. Likewise, if you laughed so much you weed

yourself, then please warn others to wear their incontinence pants before starting it!
Thank you.

Other titles from Chauffour Books

A Parrot in my soup – Andy Frazier

Imagine setting up a new life, in a warm climate, where everything is cheaper. Sounds like heaven doesn't it? But is it…?

Here's a fact. No matter where you are in the world, there will always be something wrong, if you look hard enough.

Andy Frazier moved to France 5 years ago, exchanging his rat-race life in corporate business, for one in a big old farmhouse in a rural little village, along with his partner, a selection of interesting animals and some power-tools. By day, he earns a modest living as a writer. Generally, he is happy.

But often he complains. Sometimes he even rants. Because the whole world is crammed full of annoying things.

This hilarious book is a look at the world around him over a two year period, as Andy has a pop at everything from the red wine and red politics to the price of sandwiches.

Kindle version: Amazon ABSIN: B0065HUOEE

Andy Frazier

A Parrot in my soup on Amazon UK

Who the Heck is Auntie Florette

Do you ever open your eyes in the morning, and lie there wondering how you got here? I am not referring to being in a strange bed, just in a strange world. When you turn on the radio, or the TV news, or open a paper, do you wonder at the madness of it all? Does the complete lack of common sense make you want to run away and hide? Andy Frazier's life has been a well trodden path. Growing up on a farm, running an array of businesses, firstly in agriculture, then in all sorts of random things to do with computers, all he really wanted to do was spend time with his sheep.
One day he woke up and realised the world no longer made sense, and that it probably hadn't done for some time. So he ran away and hid.

Thankfully, he gathered the love of a good woman enroute before setting up camp in South West France, in an old farmhouse with see-through walls and a few acres. At last he found peace - apart from the noise of a concrete mixer and hammer drill – where he could while away some hours doing something different.
Since that day, Andy has eeked out a meagre living writing children's books, as well as writing a monthly column for a UK magazine.

Andy Frazier

'Who the heck is Auntie Florette' is the second book containing the author's thoughts on life in rural France compared to that back in his home village of Rock in the UK over a one year period.

He is still ranting or complaining about just about everything, only he is now a year older and slightly more grumpy.

Who the Heck is Auntie Florette - on Amazon UK

The **Right Colour** – Andy Frazier

THE RIGHT COLOUR is a novel about a cow. Born on a small farm in Aberdeenshire in the mid 1980's, the Princess never really fitted in. Sure she was black, but the wrong kind of black. Her early years were plagued with hardship, bullying and racism but this only lead her to believe that she was special, the Chosen One. Now nearing the end of her life, the Princess tells her own extraordinary tale of an exceptional journey towards her destiny at the greatest cattle show of all, Royal Smithfield. On the way she encounters some colourful characters of that time, many of whom get a kick in the shin. Her exploits include a stupid sheepdog, getting drunk and a London bus, to name but a few. Her tale is entertaining, charming, funny and emotional, a good read for all age groups.

However, this book also has an underlying aim to recount, with some accuracy, the dark art of livestock showing, a world that only a lucky few have experienced. If you are one of these select few, then you will definitely relate to this story on many levels, I promise you. If you were ever at Smithfield, this book will bring back the sounds, smells and visions of those heady December days in Earls Court. If you are not, well it will reveal to you a whole new world of trials, heartaches and passion that you were blissfully unaware of.

The Right Colour on Amazon UK

I use my thumbs as a yardstick – Andy Frazier

I USE MY THUMBS AS A YARDSTICK is a true biography of a farmer who grew up during the war. Always someone looking for progress, this man was never satisfied with current farming techniques and has been a pioneer for most of his life. He also just happens, by pure coincidence, to be the author's father. He is quite proud of that.

Andy Frazier

For younger readers

Princess the cow series – by Andy Frazier

Titles in the series are:

Book 1 - **About a cow**
Princess is a young half-breed calf who grows up through hardship and bullying on a farm in Scotland. When her best friend dies her life gets set on a mission towards one destiny, the Great Royal Show. By pure chance she meets someone capable of helping her fulfil that dream.

Book 2 - **In the company of animals**
Having been sold to a man who rents animals out for money, Princess is kept in prison-like conditions. She meets some new pals and they form a lasting friendship as they plan their escape and a bid for freedom.

Book 3 – **Cow Factor**

Princess has always strived for fame and stardom and her big chance comes when she her and her pals get chance to compete on a TV talent show. But not everyone wants her to win.

Book 4 – **The Royal Detective**

Princess and her pals get a part as extras in a film about a Prince who is kidnapped. But during the film one of her friends disappears and Princess and her trusty sergeant become detectives themselves as they set off to find their friend and solve a mystery.

Other children's stories from Andy Frazier include:

BEALES CORNER

Tom hears his granddad's stories but he doesn't really listen; his summer visits are just a break for himself, he has enough troubles of his own. When the old man asks him to help him record some of his memories he is not really interested; the past is in the past and that is where it should stay. If only it would..?

MOULIN

When Henry Harman's father buys an old windmill in France, he and his little brother think it might be a nice adventure. But up in the roof of the windmill lives an old owl that the locals refer to as the Protector. But what is he protecting and why won't any of the builders go inside the building. When Henry does manage to get up into the roof, he discovers an ancient diary written by a boy 850 years earlier. The boy says he knows a secret, one so dangerous that he dare not write it down. As Henry and his brother decipher the code, things start to fall into place and they set out on an adventure of a lifetime. But can they get home again…?

Andy Frazier

IN BED WITH COWS – Cover art by Theressa McCracken.

http://www.mchumor.com/

Andy Frazier contact details:

Website: www.andyfrazier.co.uk

Follow me on Facebook: **andyfrazierbooks**

Or on Twitter: @andy_the_author

My blog: http://andyfrazierbooks.blogspot.fr/

All book titles available in ebook and paperback from Amazon UK & US stores.

Published by Chauffour Books, France

www.chauffourbooks.co.uk

You might also like to visit our global ebook store called **CountryWord**

www.countryword.com

If you register online, you will receive free weekly ebooks from a host of independent authors.

Andy Frazier

In Bed With Cows

Printed in Great Britain
by Amazon.co.uk, Ltd.,
Marston Gate.